CW00972145

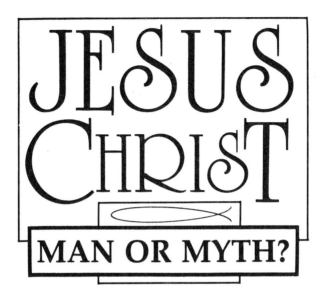

JESUS CHRIST
MAN OR MYTH?

by
E. M. Blaiklock

Thomas Nelson Publishers
Nashville • Camden • New York

Contents

1

Surviving Literature from the First Century

The desperate attempt to eliminate the historic figure of Jesus. The paucity of surviving contemporary literature in the relevant decades of the first century. Evidence of awareness of Christianity in the surviving literature at the end of the century.

'AWAY WITH HIM'

The name of Jesus has filled nineteen centuries of history. In one of those strange prophecies which sceptics have alleged was 'put into His mouth' long after the event, He remarked that He would prove a divider of men. And so, alone of all names, His has proved to be. He has haunted the minds of men as a magnificent obsession or the object of unreasoning hostility. Fascinated, His first disciples left all to follow Him. His first foes flouted justice, cast humanity aside, and scorned the majesty of law to be rid of Him at all costs.

Up and down the lands of the empire, men heard of Him, simply heard of Him, and faced everything hate or tyranny could do to be loyal to Him. The rift He had caused in Palestine lengthened and cut through the world. The empire, tolerant of all religions, banned His alone. In a century when Christians were dying for their faith, some Praetorian soldier scratched a cartoon of a

7

crucified ass upon a wall and underneath wrote, 'Alexamenos worships his god'. A small figure stands in a pose of adoration close by.

Times change. Habits change. Nations and men disastrously forget their history. They never forget Jesus of Nazareth. He still inspires love stronger than death. No century has seen more martyrs than this. He still stirs the desire to be rid of His haunting challenge, to deny the claims that He ever was, or, if He was, to prove that He was not as His followers proclaimed Him. He is shown in rock opera and film as men strive to bring this extraordinary Person down to the common level. 'Are You what You say You are?' they plead, then close their ears. But the answer remains the same.

In recent years, activity to banish or diminish Him has been unparalleled. A Hebraist of some standing, J. M. Allegro, in his expensive book of fantasy disposed of all historical evidence in such bizarre fashion that he earned the distinction of a public rebuke from several outstanding British scholars in the leading newspaper of the United Kingdom.*

---

*J. M. Allegro, *The Sacred Mushroom and the Cross* (Chellaston, Derby, England: Citadel). The devastating comment in the *London Times* was dated May 23, 1970. It ran as follows:

From Professor Sir Godfrey Driver, F.B.A. and others:

Sir,

A good deal of publicity has recently been given to a book (*The Sacred Mushroom and the Cross*) by Mr. J. M. Allegro, formerly a lecturer at Manchester University.

This is a work upon which scholars would not normally wish to comment. But the undersigned, specialists in a number of relevant disciplines and men of several faiths and none, feel it their duty to let it be known that the book is not based on any philological or other evidence which they can regard as scholarly.

In their view this work is an essay in fantasy rather than philology.

This letter was signed by G. R. Driver, Professor Emeritus of Semitic Philology, Oxford University; P. R. Ackroyd, Professor of Old Testament

Like failure has attended the quest for the historical Jesus, begun long ago in the presupposition that He could not possibly be what He said He was. From Albert Schweitzer to Rudolph Bultmann, the investigation, passing from one oddity to another, has been carried on in a spirit of such scepticism that it has recently begun to provoke the quiet amusement of secular historians.†

It would be difficult to unearth a parallel for this obstinate desire to obliterate a name. It is recorded that Thutmose III of Egypt's Eighteenth Dynasty, free at last to play the Pharaoh when the redoubtable Princess

Studies, London University; G. W. Anderson, Professor of Old Testament, Edinburgh University; J. N. D. Anderson, Professor of Oriental Laws, London University; James Barr, Professor of Semitic Languages, Manchester University; C. F. Beckingham, Professor of Islamic Studies, London University; Henry Chadwick, Dean of Christ Church, Oxford University; John Emerton, Regius Professor of Hebrew, Cambridge University; O. R. Gurney, Professor of Assyriology, Oxford University; E. G. Parrinder, Reader in Comparative Study of Religions, London University; J. B. Segal, Professor of Semitic Languages, London University; D. Winton Thomas, Emeritus Professor of Hebrew, Cambridge University; Edward Ullendorff, Professor of Ethiopian Studies, London University; G. Vermes, Reader in Jewish Studies, Oxford University; and D. J. Wiseman, Professor of Assyriology, London University.

†Observe the irony of A. N. Sherwin-White in the 'Sarum Lectures of 1960–61'.

> It is astonishing that while Graeco-Roman historians have been growing in confidence, the twentieth-century study of the Gospel narratives, starting from no less promising material, has taken so gloomy a turn in the development of form criticism that the more advanced exponents of it apparently maintain—so far as an amateur can understand the matter—that the historical Jesus is unknowable and the history of his mission cannot be written. This seems very curious when one compares the case for the best-known contemporary of Christ, who like Christ is a well-documented figure—Tiberius Caesar.

A. N. Sherwin-White, *Roman Society and Roman Law in the New Testament* (Oxford, 1963), p. 187.

Hatshepsut died, made a savage attempt with hammer, chisel, and sheathing stone to blot out all record of this relative who had overshadowed him. He failed. The spiteful masonry around the Karnak obelisk fell away and revealed the royal name. Thutmose's malice died with him.[1]

Why the unease over an historical Jesus? It cannot simply be a scholar's zeal for truth. Julius Caesar is not thus dismissed, or his rather unsuccessful reconnaissance across the English Channel relegated to legend, despite the fact that our principal informant is Julius himself (in a book designed to secure his political reputation) and that confirmatory evidence of that campaign consists merely of a shield in the river at the Chelsea crossing of the Thames, a few lines in Cicero's voluminous correspondence,[2] and only a handful of later references.

It is difficult to lose from history one who has truly lived. Personalities appear and are listed confidently as real with little but a half-forgotten name, a profile on a coin, or a fragmentary inscription to authenticate their existence. The quarter of Alexander's empire which lay toward the east in Bactria and India is known only from archaeological and numismatic records; many of its rulers are named and their actual existence unquestioned. Ancient history would provide similar illustrations of persons and events, slenderly documented, which provoke no great enthusiasm to refute and obliterate. Why this widespread desire to be rid of Jesus?

Perhaps there is an answer blowing in the wind, or at least rising unbidden in the mind: 'Why, what evil has He done?' 'Away with Him! Crucify.' 'Shall I crucify your King?' Or was Bunyan near the truth? 'Then said Mr. No-Good, "Away with such a fellow from the earth." "Ay," said Mr. Malice, "for I hate the very sight of him." "Let us despatch him out of the way," said Mr. Hate-Light.'³ The jury of Vanity Fair has often been in session from the days of Caiaphas' Sanhedrin and Demetrius' guild of Ephesian silversmiths to the events of today.

Could it be that there are always those irked under the thrust and pressure of Jesus Christ's commanding Person or searched and raked by His words who seek comfort in some hope that the records were falsified? In this hope of a delusion exposed, they turn the attack upon the historicity of Jesus. Christianity triumphed over its most serious opponent, the soldiers' worship of the soldierly Mithras, largely because Christianity could oppose to the legendary Mithras the historical reality of Christ. It is necessarily at Him that those aim their shafts who indulge the strange death-wish that life is 'all sound and fury, signifying nothing,' and a hole in the damp turf the final escape.

Such assurance, comfortable or otherwise, is elusive. Quite apart from the question whether the behests of Christ are accepted or scorned, and whether that astonishingly documented story of the empty tomb is believed or disbelieved, it remains true that no responsible historian can dismiss the historical reality of Jesus. Moreover, in spite of some biblical expositors who can accommodate a scepticism, which was once less improperly exercised outside the church, to the continued occupation of posts of responsibility inside the church, Jesus lived according to the proportions which the New Testament sets forth—no self-deluded, tragic failure, no invention of enthusiasts, but the most extraordinary being who ever trod the earth. Nineteen centuries of history have been influenced and penetrated by Him. As the brilliant Frenchman Ernest Renan, one of the forerunners of sceptical New Testament criticism and himself no Christian, remarked in a famous peroration, Jesus Christ has been 'so completely the cornerstone of humanity that to tear His name from this world, would be to shake it to its foundations'.[4] Most students of history would abandon their quest for truth if it could be proved that the record of events which affect almost two millennia arose from the naive delusions or criminal deceptions of a band of simple Jews, who created out of nothing native to their minds the whole transforming story.

CONTEMPORARY LITERATURE

The New Testament, of course, is the chief literary source for the life and work of Jesus Christ, and to that mass of monumental evidence the theme must soon return. To say, as J. M. Allegro somewhere does, that 'there is no worthwhile contemporary evidence outside the New Testament that Jesus ever existed,' is no true contribution to discussion. The four words *outside the New Testament* strip the assertion of meaning. Historians would be glad to have such authentic, multiple, congruent evidence on more personalities and events of ancient history.

What do we mean by 'contemporary evidence'? It is a sombre fact that practically everything written during the lifetime of Christ has perished. Parts of one unimportant historical work survive from the years of His ministry or their vicinity. The badly written history of Rome by Velleius Paterculus, a retired army officer of Tiberius turned amateur historian, was published in A.D. 30. The procuratorial records of Palestine were much less likely to be preserved. Two-thirds of Pilate's name has recently been found in an inscription at Caesarea along with a reference in one word to a shrine of Tiberius—an oddly brief authentication of the procurator and his preoccupations. Jesus is authenticated in no other way, outside the gospels, save by Josephus and a sentence in a Roman historian. Such has been time's destruction. The decade of the forties has left little, save that the pleasant fables of the Macedonian freedman, Phaedrus, were written during those years.

The same remark is almost true of the surviving literature of the fifties and sixties of the first century, when the first three gospels, and most of the letters of the New Testament were being written. Bookends set a foot apart on this desk where I write would enclose the works from those significant years. Curiously, much of it comes from Spanish emigrants in Rome, a foretaste of what the Iberian peninsula was to give to her conqueror—senators, writers, and two important emperors, Trajan and Hadrian. Paul had foresight when he set a visit to Spain in his program.

The full list of Spanish contributions from the decade of Nero's principate, in which Christians first attracted official attention, is interesting.[5] Caught like Paul in that evil tangle of events, and destined for death like Nero's Christian victims, were the philosopher, writer and statesman, Seneca, and his nephew, the poet Lucan. Seneca was the most considerable figure in Roman letters since the great literary flowering of the Augustan Age. He was born at Corduba about the time of the nativity, won wealth and station (judging neither inconsistent with philosophy), suffered exile under Claudius (rather unphilosophically endured), and returned to Rome to serve as tutor to the youthful Nero. This was in A.D. 49. During Nero's early years Seneca, in partnership

with Burrus, the bluff commandant of the household
troops, gave the Roman world five years of good admi-
nistration which became legendary. In the early sixties,
horrified by Nero's mounting license, Seneca retired to
write his philosophical treatises and letters, works of
noble worth which may be dated round 63 and 64.
Seneca died in Nero's Terror of 65 which, like Hitler's
fierce reprisals after the Bomb Plot, was launched on
Rome's upper class when a conspiracy, clumsily
mounted by one Calpurnius Piso, failed. The story of
Nero's mad years and Seneca's death is told vividly in
Tacitus' *Annales*.[6] We possess quite a sturdy volume of
Seneca's writings. They are a fine contribution to Roman
literature, a monument of what is called 'Silver Latin'.

Seneca's nephew, the precocious twenty-six-year-old
poet Lucan, died in the same tragic aftermath of the
Pisonian conspiracy. We still have his long poem on the
century-old civil war between Julius Caesar and
Pompey. Its competent verse fatally roused Nero's
artistic jealousy, and no more than such a provocation
was needed to earn a death sentence from that vulgar
sadist.

A third and luckier Spaniard was an old soldier named
Columella. He had actually served in Syria during the
years which saw Pilate's recall from Judea and the
establishment of the church at Antioch. Twenty-five
miles from Rome, at Ardea, he took up farming, like
many an old soldier, and in A.D. 60 published a book on
agriculture.

Another writer, better known to the modern world
because of Henry Sienkiewicz's brilliant novel *Quo Vadis*
and the striking (though historically faulty) film made
from it, is Gaius Petronius. This indolent aristocrat was
murdered in A.D. 66 by Tigellinus, Nero's evil com-

mander of the Praetorian guard. Petronius was a notorious voluptuary, though he proved an able governor of Bithynia. He earned the nickname of 'Arbiter Elegantiarum' (judge in matters of taste) from his competent direction of the young Nero's pleasures. Petronius wrote *Satyricon*, the only novel from his century known to us. Large fragments tell of the disreputable doings of three Greek scamps in the Campanian seaports. We see in the *Satyricon*, as this romance is called, the common life of Italy in slum and market-place in that age of money-making and vulgarity, of crime and lowered standards of morality—the proletariat, to be discovered elsewhere in the writings of that decade except in the first five books of the New Testament.

The list is now almost complete. The satirist Persius died in A.D. 62 at the age of twenty-eight, a delicate young man and the victim, no doubt, of Rome's malarial climate. We have a few hundred lines of his laboured verse. There was also the man called the Elder Pliny, to distinguish him from his nephew, Pliny the letter-writer, of whom more will be said in the next chapter. This able man, a soldier and later an admiral of the fleet, has left us a mass of books called *Historia Naturalis*, a collection of odd facts about the world of nature and built out of the same sort of academic diligence shown by Benjamin Disraeli's father, the bibliophil Isaac Disraeli, in his daily fossicking in the British Museum. Pliny died of heart failure, the victim of his lively curiosity, at the time of the eruption of Vesuvius in A.D. 79. There are only two remaining extant authors. Asconius Pedianus became blind in A.D. 64. Some fragments of his commentary on Cicero survive. Quintus Curtius may have been busy on his history of Alexander the Great during this time. Both are minor figures of literature, unknown save to specialist scholars.

Of this handful of writers would any have been likely
to mention Christ? Perhaps Seneca, if in fact he met and
talked with Paul. But there is small likelihood that this
pleasant medieval legend is true. Besides, in A.D. 64, in
the summer of which year Nero took hostile note of
Rome's Christians, Seneca was a distracted and tormented man. A year later he was dead, driven to suicide
by the mad young tyrant whom he had sought in vain to
tame.

LATER LITERATURE

The seventies saw stable government in Rome again,
under the Flavian dynasty, whose founder, Vespasian,
had emerged victorious from the shocking events of
A.D. 68 and 69, which saw the suicide of Nero, and four
contestants for his principate locked in quadrilateral civil
war. Little literature survives from the period, but
consider the few surviving publications, and ask whether
one dead in Palestine forty years before, or his less
remote but scattered, decimated Roman followers, would
have been likely to find mention. Tacitus, destined to be
a great historian and a greater stylist, published a minor
work on oratory in A.D. 81. Martial, another Spaniard,
was writing epigrams. Hundreds of these witty poems
survive from the seventies and eighties—clever, sometimes scurrilous, often brilliant. He does not clearly
mention the Christians, but how many were alive or left
in Rome after that searching assault on the church in
A.D. 64?

The nineties saw the last flowering of the 'Silver Age'
of Latin literature. Quintilian, yet another Spaniard,
published his twelve books on oratory in A.D. 95. This is
an interesting date, for it was about that time that the

fourth gospel was written. Statius, the poet, had already published *Silvae*. Tacitus commenced his fine historical work in A.D. 98 with two small books. One was a monograph on his father-in-law, Agricola, who had governed Britain in the late seventies and carried Roman reconnaisance cautiously to Scotland. It was one of the very few biographies to come from the literature of the ancient world. The other monograph was a book on Germany. Would Quintilian or Tacitus be likely to mention Christ or the church in such works?

Juvenal, Martial's friend, had hardly begun to write before the end of the century. Like Martial's poems, his mordant, satiric writings touch life at various levels and from many wry angles. He mentions scornfully the Jews, whose shanty town was evident outside the walls of Rome, but he does not mention the Christians. Could one expect him to know them? Their faith was proscribed. They sought to escape attention. Satirists fasten on absurdities thrust on their notice, and Juvenal found enough absurdities in Rome.

Tacitus must have begun writing his historical works of greater note as soon as the tyrant Domitian died. This was in A.D. 95 when John published, or had recently published, his gospel. Tacitus's *Historiae*, written early in the second century, deal with the year A.D. 69 and inevitably mention the ghastly Jewish war. His *Annales*, which pick up the story of the emperors at Augustus's death, were given to the world in A.D. 116. Large portions of both these fine historical works remain. The *Annales* gives a detailed account of Nero's persecution of the Christians of Rome which began in the closing weeks of July 64. It is a highly prejudiced account, accepting the slanders which so vividly reveal the basis of persecution of the Christians in the first century, but it mentions

Christ and His suffering under Pontius Pilatus, Tiberius' procurator of Judea. We shall return to this passage later.

A friend of Tacitus was Pliny, the nephew of the old scholar who died in the eruption of Vesuvius. Pliny, like Petronius, once governed Bithynia and in the years A.D. 110 to 112 wrote for advice to the emperor Trajan concerning the church which almost had the province in its grip. Pliny's spies and investigations provided the governor with some accurate information about the origin and practices of the church (quoted in the next chapter), but failed to confirm the slanders which Tacitus, a few years before, had put too uncritically into his powerful Latin. We shall not add Suetonius to the list. Though Suetonius has a garbled reference to Christ, he wrote after A.D. 120. It suffices for our present purpose to halt within a generation of the death of the last witness to the living Jesus.

Two of the four major writers of Rome, whose works survive from the generation in which John's literary activity falls, do mention the church and its Master. The quibble of J. M. Allegro and other critics, that a figure so significant as Christians claim their Lord to have been would have set contemporary writers talking, is thus seen in its absurdity. It is remarkable that Christianity, which probably reached Rome in the forties of the century,‡ should, in fact, have so rapidly commanded attention and found mention in relevant literature. We shall next examine those references more closely, and then turn to Flavius Josephus, the clever Jewish priest who became secretary to the emperor Vespasian and wrote in Greek the story of his people and their bitter clash with Rome.

---

‡Such is the inference if the Nazareth Decree is dated correctly in the principate of Claudius. See E. M. Blaiklock, *Archaeology of the New Testament* (Grand Rapids: Zondervan, 1970), pp. 77–83.

2
Testimony of Tacitus, Pliny and Josephus

Tacitus and Pliny and the Christians. Josephus and Christ. The new awareness of the worth of Josephus.

TWO NOBLE ROMANS

We must now turn with somewhat closer attention to the two Roman senators and writers, Tacitus and Pliny, literary contemporaries of John, who make reference to the Christians and their Lord. Cornelius Tacitus was probably of north Italian stock, as were others of Rome's best writers, and was born somewhere near A.D. 55. He began his senatorial career under Vespasian. He witnessed a few years of Domitian's tyranny, held the office of consul, and was proconsul of Asia in the years A.D. 112 and 113 just after his friend Pliny served in similar fashion in Bithynia. Tacitus was a notable orator. He must have died sometime after A.D. 116.

Gaius Plinius Caecilius Secundus was born about A.D. 61 and died after two years of office as legate of Bithynia, around A.D. 110. Pliny, the Younger, as he is popularly called, was another north Italian, from Comum, a successful lawyer, a polished gentleman and diplomat. He wrote, in distinguished Latin, letters of great social and historical interest. We must look at the relevant pages of each writer in turn.

TACITUS AND THE CHRISTIANS OF ROME

The *Annales* of Tacitus were published somewhere near A.D. 116. Tacitus was a careful writer and collected his raw material with diligence. We have two letters, for example, of his friend Pliny, giving a vivid, eyewitness account of the eruption of Vesuvius in August, A.D. 79, written in response to an inquiry of the historian who was busy with the book of the *Historiae*, now lost, which covered that year. As a boy living on the Bay of Naples, Pliny witnessed the eruption. In the early years of the second century, there would have been many who could tell Tacitus from personal experience how Nero came to persecute and proscribe the church. His informants must have given a highly biased and critical account. Tacitus wrote it in the Fifteenth Book of the *Annales*.

Tacitus told how a fire broke out not far from Rome's Capena Gate on July 19, A.D. 64. Gaining rapid hold among the booths and hovels of the crowded trading quarters around the great circus under the Palatine and Caelian Hills, the conflagration raged for six days and seven nights. Of the fourteen regions into which Augustus had divided the city, three were completely wiped out, and only four remained untouched. The loss of life was heavy.

To the stunned population the question of responsibility immediately suggested itself. Who was to blame? Surely somebody? The historian makes it quite clear that a grim suspicion circulated. Had Nero himself done the deed? It is certain that the young emperor could not be charged with inertia. He had rushed from Antium where he was on holiday, opened the public buildings and imperial gardens to the homeless, requisitioned food and materials, and thrown all his energies into the task of relief. Nevertheless a rumour was abroad. It was alleged that, in the midst of the catastrophe, Nero, dilettante and poseur, had ascended an eminence, the so-called tower of Maecenas, whence the terrifying sight could be seen in all its awful splendour and, lyre in hand, had sung of the fall of Troy. It was also remarked that the devastation was not without its convenience for one whose megalomaniac building schemes sought space for his vast Golden House.

The truth will never be known. Nero, lyre changed to fiddle, has come down the centuries in a proverb, but if those heavy features hid the secret of Rome's conflagration, the secret perished with the young criminal five years later, and his accomplices held their peace. It is a fact, nonetheless, that Nero was terrified. The proletariat of Rome could be dangerous. Nero met the menace with a parade of religion, the consultation of oracles, public prayer and sacrifices, but popular emotion refused to be appeased. Some impressive demonstration seemed necessary, and at this point some villain who had the emperor's ear conceived a dastardly idea. Let Tacitus tell the story.

> Such were the various forms of relief suggested by human planning. Then means were taken to propitiate the gods. The Sibylline books were consulted, and prayers were offered, as the books prescribed, to Vulcan, to Ceres, and to Prosperine. Juno was supplicated by the matrons, first on the Capitol, and afterwards at the nearest point upon the sea coast, from which water was drawn to sprinkle the temple and image of the goddess; banquets to the goddesses and all-night festivals were celebrated by married women.
>
> But neither the aid of men, nor the emperor's bounty, nor propitiatory offerings to the gods, could remove the grim suspicion that the fire had been started by Nero's order. To put an end to this rumour, he shifted the charge on to others, and inflicted the most cruel tortures upon a group of people

detested for their abominations, and popularly known as 'Christians'. This name came from one Christus, who was put to death in the principate of Tiberius by the Procurator Pontius Pilate. Though checked for a time, the destructive superstition broke out again, not in Judaea only, where its mischief began, but even in Rome, where every abominable and shameful iniquity, from all the world, pours in and finds a welcome.

First those who acknowledged themselves of this sect were arrested; and upon their testimony a large number were condemned, not so much on the charge of arson, as for their hatred of the human race. Their death was turned into an entertainment. They were clothed in the skins of wild beasts, and torn to pieces by dogs; they were crucified or staked up to be burned, to serve the purpose of lamps when daylight failed. Nero gave up his own gardens for this spectacle; he provided also games, during which he mingled with the crowd, or rode round upon a chariot, in the garb of a charioteer. But guilty as these people were and worthy of direst punishment, the fact that they were being cut off for no public good, but only to glut the cruelty of one man, aroused a feeling of pity.[1]

In such fashion the Christians entered Roman history, tormented, scorned and misrepresented by the most powerfully mordant of Rome's historians. Tacitus alleged that they hated the human race and that their faith was a 'destructive superstition'. The expression suggests the social misfit, unable by temperament or unwilling by conviction to participate in the common activities of a community. The mob hated them. An uncompromising conscience had withdrawn the followers of Christ from participation in many of the activities of a society which was much more communal and closely knit than that of the Anglo-Saxon world of today. The crowd had marked the abstinence, reacted as crowds do react, and branded the abstainers with disapproval. Crowds are feeble in reasoning and passionate in imagination. Hence, too often, the sad fate of minorities.

Nero, like a hundred demagogues before and after him,
seized on the ill-considered emotions of the mass. There
was fuel for Nero's firing in the dislike which the
compliant and conforming majority feel for the dissident
and nonconforming few. The spectacle of moral earnest-
ness offends the morally inert, and the sight of dis-
ciplined living rebukes and angers self-indulgence. The
vested interests of vice fear virtue, and corruption is
uneasy in the presence of uprightness. Christians stirred
the emotional hostility of the ancient crowd. Nero canal-
ized the crowd's passion, gave it self-expression, supplied
a cover of logic for baseness and a cloak of social
righteousness for unreasoning hatred.

But in that is a study of mass psychology and human
evil outside our present theme, or we might proceed to
the study of another public outburst recorded in Acts 19.

In Tacitus we have a great writer, a man of massive
intelligence, recording the memories of an act of wickedness described to him by those who could remember the
middle and the later years of Nero's principate. Observe
that they used the name of Christ and assigned Him to
his time and place. This is the significance of the account
in the context of our present argument. The bulk of the
New Testament was appearing during the years of the
informants' active recollection. In any sphere of history,
this should be sufficient for unquestioned confidence in
the historicity of an individual. There can be no possible
question of Christian tampering with the evidence:
Tacitus wrote those words.

PLINY AND THE CHRISTIANS OF BITHYNIA

We turn now to the next item of historical evidence. In
the year A.D. 111, the governor of Bithynia, Caius

Caecilius Plinius Secundus, became aware of tension in his province. As an experienced treasury official with some special knowledge of the region, Pliny had been the obvious choice when Trajan decided to place Bithynia under an imperial legate. He was a capable man, uncommonly alert for events of importance. The Christian church, strong and deeply established, was striking heavily at the roots of Bithynian paganism, and protests were finding expression. Trade was suffering (see Acts 19 for a similar reaction that took place in Ephesus), and the governor, anxious for peace, prosperity, and especially financial stability, took action. Pliny was in the habit of consulting the emperor Trajan on all matters of importance, and this official correspondence has survived as Volume Ten of Pliny's fascinating correspondence. The letter of Pliny and the imperial reply form the record of an act of repression. The letter should be read carefully, both for its poignant story of ancient suffering and for the light it throws on the deep motives of persecution. Above all, it clearly establishes, at a high official level, the historicity of Jesus. Pliny wrote:

> It is a rule, Sir, which I invariably observe, to refer myself to you in all my doubts; for who is more capable of guiding my uncertainty or informing my ignorance? Having never been present at any trials of the Christians, I am unacquainted with the method and limits to be observed either in examining or punishing them, whether any difference is to be made on account of age, or no distinction allowed between the youngest and the adult; whether repentance admits to a pardon, or if a man has been once a Christian it avails him nothing to recant; whether the mere profession of Christianity, albeit without the commission of crimes, or only the charges associated therewith are punishable—on all these points I am in considerable perplexity.

In the meantime, the method I have observed towards those who have been denounced to me as Christians in this: I interrogated them whether they were in fact Christians; if they confessed it, I repeated the question twice, adding the threat of capital punishment; if they still persevered, I ordered them to be executed. For whatever the nature of their beliefs might be, I could at least feel no doubt that determined contumacy and inflexible obstinacy deserved chastisement. There were others also possessed with the same infatuation, but being citizens of Rome, I directed them to be taken to Rome for trial.

These accusations spread (as is usually the case) from the mere fact of the matter being investigated, and several forms of the mischief came to light. A placard was put up, without any signature, accusing a large number of persons by name. Those who denied they were, or had ever been, Christians, and who repeated after me an invocation to the gods, and offered formal worship with libation and frankincense, before your statue, which I had ordered to be brought into Court for that purpose, together with those of the gods, and who finally cursed Christ —none of which acts, it is said, those who are really Christians can be forced into performing—these I thought it proper to discharge. Others who were named by the anonymous informer at first confessed themselves Christians, and then denied it; true, they said, they had been of that persuasion but they had quitted it, some three years, others many years, and a few as much as twenty-five years previously. They all worshipped your statue and the images of the gods, and cursed Christ.

They affirmed, however, that the whole of their guilt, or their error, was that they were in the habit of meeting on a certain fixed day before it was light, when they sang in alternate verses a hymn to Christ, as to a god, and bound themselves by a solemn oath, not to perform any wicked deed, but never to commit any fraud, theft or adultery, never to falsify their word, nor deny a trust when they should be called upon to make it good; after which it was their custom to separate, and then reassemble to partake of food—but food of an ordinary and innocent kind. Even this practice, however, they had abandoned after the publication of my edict, by which, according to your orders, I had forbidden political associations. I therefore judged it so much the more necessary to extract the real truth, with the assistance of torture, from two female slaves, who were styled deaconesses: but I could discover nothing more than depraved and excessive superstition.

I therefore adjourned the proceedings, and betook myself at once to your counsel. For the matter seemed to me well worth referring to you—especially considering the numbers endangered. Persons of all ranks and ages, and of both sexes are, and will be, involved in the prosecution. For this contagious superstition is not confined to the cities only, but has spread through the villages and rural districts, it seems possible, however, to check and cure it. It is certain at least that the temples, which had been almost deserted, begin now to be frequented; and the sacred festivals, after a long intermission, are again revived; while there is a general demand for sacrificial meat, which for some time past had met with but few purchasers. From hence it is easy to imagine what multitudes may be reclaimed from this error, if a door be left open to repentance.[2]

It is easy to reconstruct the situation. Pliny, preoccupied with provincial finances, had received complaints from the temple priests, the guild of the butchers whose sales of sacrificial meat were falling off, and from all the small community which derived profit from the smooth functioning of pagan ritual. The Christians were tampering with the established processes of life, challenging, rebuking. In Rome, as in Ephesus where the tourist trade was harmed, the injured forces of paganism struck back with some success. The weak and the fearful fell away. The faithful and the brave died or suffered exile. Sales of sacrificial meat increased, and the anxious governor saw his disturbed province sink to rest. In his letter he left a record of one of the precise moments when social ostracism of the Christian church turned into state persecution. Above all, in light of the present theme, he left a precisely dated record of the church and a clear mention of Christ.

The last book of the New Testament had been written a score of years before Pliny penned the careful letters to his prince. The long years of state persecution were about to begin. They were to cleanse and purify the church. But the church could never have survived the impact of those years had there not been in her midst a body of men and women who literally counted all things loss for Christ. We must bow our heads before those who endured all the human heart finds difficult to bear in order to preserve the faith unsullied, unadulterated, undamaged and intact.

And those were the men who remembered, or had heard from their immediate forbears, the oral tradition, and perhaps seen the written testimony of those who knew the apostles, if not the apostles themselves. Paul was prevented from evangelizing Bithynia (Ac 16:7), but that task must have been undertaken with vigour long before the end of the first century for the faith to hold the area so completely by the close of the first decade of the second century.

No shadow of doubt could have been in the minds of the first Bithynian Christians concerning the historicity of Jesus Christ, and that confidence ran in a very brief and strongly linked chain to the Person of the Lord Himself.

JOSEPHUS AND CHRIST

A third area of contemporary historical evidence must at this point be considered—that of Flavius Josephus. Josephus was a shrewd Jewish priest who was opposed to the fiercely nationalistic policies which led to the disastrous clash with Rome in A.D. 66. He was, nevertheless, given the governorship of Galilee and, if we are to believe his own naturally prejudiced account, defended the region with vigour against the Roman military penetration led by Vespasian and Titus. He was captured in A.D. 67, having cleverly extricated himself from a suicide pact entered into by a group of defeated guerillas cornered in a cave.

Josephus, or Joseph as he still was called among the Jews, had been to Rome in A.D. 63 and 64 as a young man of some twenty-five years. Perhaps he had shrewdly summed up the political situation there and had noted over the succeeding years the gathering power of the frontier armies, that mortal danger to the stability of Rome. At any rate, taken prisoner and brought before Vespasian, he cleverly saved his liberty and his future by boldly prophesying that Vespasian and his son Titus were to be emperors of Rome.[3] Joseph so impressed the Roman general by his prophecy, that he was kept at headquarters under special surveillance. When, at the end of the sanguinary year A.D. 69, Vespasian emerged from multilateral civil war, as the ruler of Rome, the clever Joseph was latinized into Flavius Josephus, Flavius being the new ruler's household name, and given a pension in the imperial household. His future security was assured.

He set to work to write about his people and produced, in rather graceless Greek, major works of history in the late seventies and in the early nineties of the century. The second work, the *Antiquities of the Jews* published at the very time when John was writing his gospel, contains a curious passage about Christ which many have alleged to be an interpolation. Translated literally, it runs:

> About this time there appeared Jesus, a wise man, if indeed he should be called a man, for he was the doer of surprising

works, and a teacher of such as accept the truth with pleasure. He won many Jews and many Greeks. He was the Messiah. Pilate, on the accusation of our leading men, condemned him to be crucified, but those who had first loved him did not give up. On the third day he appeared to them, living again, for God's prophets had foretold this, and countless other astonishing things about him. And the tribe of the Christians, called after him, is still in existence.[4]

R. Marcus, in the Loeb Classics translation of Josephus, comments in a long footnote on this remarkable paragraph that the text goes back to A.D. 324. It was certainly known in this expanded form by Eusebius. He concludes, 'The most probable view seems to be that our text represents substantially what Josephus wrote, but that some alterations have been made by a Christian interpolator.'[5] Responsible critics will be most ready to admit the last possibility. Had the Jewish priest written, 'He was the Messiah,' he would have thus declared himself a Christian. He probably wrote 'the so-called Messiah,' as he did when, two books later, he mentioned Christ again, in connection with the murder of James.

Allow the plausible alteration of one letter, and the passage could read, 'A teacher of such as accept the unusual with pleasure'. The phrase 'if indeed he should be called a man,' may have been given a different twist by Josephus. This is all conjecture, but allow it all, and the testimony of the non-Christian, hostile Josephus to the historicity of Jesus Christ is still inextricably tangled with his text. Whatever, in his own faith or practice, a man may do about the monumental fact, the fact itself remains — Jesus lived.

Note that it is classical, not New Testament scholarship, which provides confirmation of the core of the so-called *Flavium Testimonium*. If a personal testimony may at this point be injected, I must confess that I had myself, until recently, dismissed the passage as of doubtful authenticity and as unreliable evidence in New Testament apologetics. I discovered that colleagues in classical history had passed me by and recognized a depository of genuine information. They led me to re-examine the whole position.

Some twenty years ago an unexpected confirmation emerged. An Israeli scholar, Professor Schlomo Pines of the Hebrew University of Jerusalem, drew attention to a forgotten Arabic text of Josephus dating back to the fourth century. It is preserved in a history of the church written by Agapius, an Arab bishop of Baghdad. It would seem to be a version which antedates other known texts. Pines quotes the Arabic version in a monograph published by the Israeli Academy of Sciences and Humanities in 1971. It runs:

> Similarly Josephus, the Hebrew. For he says: 'At this time there was a wise man called Jesus, and his conduct was good, and he was known to be virtuous. And many people from among the Jews and other nations became his disciples. Pilate condemned him to be crucified and to die. And those who had become his disciples did not abandon their discipleship. They reported that he had appeared to them three days after his crucifixion and that he was alive. Accordingly, he was perhaps the Messiah concerning whom the prophets have recounted wonders.'

Professor Pines points out that the traditional version refers to Jesus as 'a wise man, if indeed one ought to call him a man,' and notes that the Arabic version simply refers to him as 'a wise man'. Also he notes that the Greek version boldly asserts that Jesus was the Messiah, while the Arabic says, 'He was perhaps the Messiah,' or according to another possible rendering of the Arabic, 'thought to be the Messiah'.

It would seem clear that the Arabic version contains a text of Josephus earlier than the contaminated text which has survived from other sources. It could be that Josephus was early translated into a Syriac version, and the Arabic derived from that. In any case, it supports the contention that, if all suspected interpolations are eliminated from the controversial text, a striking testimony to the central facts of Christianity still survives. Above all it sets Joseph, the Jewish historian, alongside the two contemporary Romans, as evidence for the existence and historical reality of Jesus. As Professor Pines remarks dryly, it is 'all the authors who consider that Jesus was a mythical rather than a historical person who regard the *Testimonium* as a Christian forgery'.

An appendix to G. A. Williamson's Penguin translation of Josephus, quoted Slavonic additions to the text, with some arguments advanced in favour of their authenticity, which lie outside our present inquiry. Josephus's testimony has been limited to one highly relevant passage, and though it is true that the Roman-Jew, unlikable as he is in person, has been accorded recently higher worth as an historian, it has not been thought necessary to widen the investigation to include more controversial material. As the lawyers say, 'The case rests'. Apart from all Christian testimony, there can be no doubt at all that Jesus was a figure of history.

3

Approaching the Synoptic Gospels

*The documents of the New Testament, their language,
nature and worth. The correct approach to them as
history. Mark, Matthew and Luke examined in turn for
content, date and testimony.*

THE GREEK NEW TESTAMENT

We must pass now to the chief source of our knowledge
of Christ, the documents in everyday Greek known as the
New Testament, and principally to the four narratives
which we call the gospels. We have established that
references to Christ and the church occupy an almost
disproportionate place in the few surviving authors of the
late first century. It is also established that, when
considered solely on the evidence of secular and non-
Christian historiography, Jesus existed as a figure of
history. To pass on to Christian literature of the time is
obviously the next step.

The New Testament documents are from nine different hands, with the variety of style to be expected from
men ranging from a Galilean fisherman to one of the
finest minds of antiquity. Their language is the basic
Greek which had become the second language of the
eastern Mediterranean. It is exactly what one would
expect from men writing to communicate with their
first-century contemporaries. Narratives, treatises and

letters are in the style, fashion and speech of the day, carry no evidence of peculiar composition, and appear to be no less than they claim to be.

The power of this common speech grows on the reader. Like myself, J. B. Phillips, the popular translator of the New Testament, approached the New Testament from the angle of a classics scholar. 'I had read the best of Classical Greek,' he says in his remarkable testimony, 'for over ten years at school and Cambridge.' As one who has read the same magnificent language and taught it in a university for over forty years, I can follow and applaud what the translator goes on to say. 'The language is not so pedestrian as I had at first supposed. Although I did my utmost to preserve an emotional detachment, I found again and again that the material under my hands was strangely alive; it spoke to my condition in the most uncanny way.'[1]

Adolf Deissmann, one of the first scholars to point out the relevance of the newly discovered Egyptian papyri to New Testament linguistic studies, had reached a similar conclusion. He expressed it in the Haskell Lectures in 1929. 'The view,' he wrote, 'that the Greek of the New Testament was the language of the common people of its time has given cause, occasionally, to the erroneous opinion that the New Testament was thereby degraded and depreciated. I can only confess that to me the New Testament has become greater and more venerable the more I have learned to regard it in close connection with the people of its day. And just from a linguistic viewpoint, a consideration of the style of the New Testament shows how important is this little book, created from such simple material, even as a literary document, in the literature of the world.'[2]

THE APPROACH

How shall the evidence contained in the New Testament be scrutinized? Perhaps it is relevant to quote J. B. Phillips again. He was drawn into a radio discussion with E. V. Rieu, a fellow classicist who had translated the gospels for the Penguin Classics. To a question from Phillips, Dr. Rieu replied, 'My personal reason was my own intense desire to satisfy myself as to the authenticity and the spiritual content of the gospels. . . . I approached them in the same spirit as I would have approached them had they been presented to me as recently discovered Greek manuscripts.' Phillips asked, 'Did you get the feeling that the whole material was extraordinarily alive?' Rieu replied, 'I got the deepest feeling. . . . My work changed me.'

This is the natural approach to the New Testament for a trained classical scholar. Here is a collection of documents. What have they to say? Who wrote them? When were they written? A classical scholar finds it difficult to be patient with some of the exotic theories of literary criticism which have bedevilled New Testament studies. Classical historians have been a little ironical in recent decades over the calculated scepticism of New Testament scholars who refuse to see what the classicists so naturally see—a record of life in the first century, if no more than that, which must at least be accorded its unique value as historical material.*

Had the so-called form critics confined their activities to that which may be a demonstration of the obvious— the part played by the experience and practice of the church in determining the stresses and emphases in material which was necessarily and admittedly selective

*See footnote p. 8.

—they might conceivably have thrown some light on the mind of the first communities of Christians. Even the rude art of the catacombs picked and chose the themes which most appealed to the embattled Christians of Italy. But when critical theory seeks to persuade that liturgical and spiritual needs and aspirations, taking shape from nowhere, and within the lifetime of those who had known the first half of the first century, themselves created a supporting literature, the narratives and sayings which form the gospels, fantasy is propounded which would provoke ridicule in any less confined and introverted sphere of literary criticism.

The gospels as documents fall into the literary pattern of their age. It is reasonable to regard them as the work of men within close reach of the events which they recorded. They were put together as books were normally put together in their time. If they are to yield any meaning, they must be judged as documents of history, written in the language of their time and place, and existing today in a quite incomparable number of ancient texts. No one can begin to understand the gospels unless they are approached as historical writing, part of the records of an age. To classify them in any other category, to study them in any other way, is to insure misunderstanding by laying down the form of the conclusion before investigation begins, and to confuse the evidence before it is examined. For a critic, on no authority but his own, to begin with a list of events which could not have happened and a catalogue of that which could not have been said is obviously to preclude all possibility of objective examination.

The documents, on E. V. Rieu's principle, quoted above, must first be approached in their existing form. The traditions which surround their authorship and origin must be considered and assessed. Only then is the investigator in a position to scrutinize the historicity of events or the reality of the person who stands out from those events. It has been maintained that He is a figure of history. It is claimed here that apart from all non-biblical evidence, on the testimony of the New Testament alone, He is a figure of history. It is also the task of the Christian documents to set forth what sort of a figure He was.

The Gospel of Mark

A glance, then, first at the three synoptic narratives beginning with the gospel of Mark, the briefest and traditionally the first to be written. It is a small book of simple, rugged Greek, from which the figure of Jesus stands forth vividly. It speaks with colloquial directness. The writer was clearly in haste to set down important events, perhaps under strong direction (2 Pe 1:12–16). The writer's haste may have been justified, for he appears to have lacked opportunity to conclude his narrative. It is commonly held that some concluding verses were by another hand and not part of an original text.

To read the book right through in its original language, fast and without translating (a prerequisite for the sound appraisal of any text in any literature) is to gain an impression of honesty and objectivity which bears indeed the ring of truth. Thus read, the text of Mark's narrative in no way suggests that the tradition about its origin and authorship is at all unreasonable. Tradition, as sensible and responsible scholarship has been steadily compelled to learn by the archaeological and historical discoveries of over a hundred years, is a repository of knowledge which must be treated with respect and never bypassed in research.

Tradition going back to Papias, through his friend Polycarp, who knew John, reports that Mark (presumably Barnabas' nephew) undertook to record the memories of Peter. Papias served in the Roman spa of Hierapolis, one of the cities in the Lycus valley with Christian cells. If he was born, as seems likely, about A.D. 60 and died about A.D. 130, there is nothing incredible in this tradition. The marks of an eyewitness are apparent on every page of the swift narrative. In Mark's language we seem to catch the accents of Peter's voice. Of all the apostles, the personality of Peter stands forth most clearly in the stories which speak of him.[3] Consider the touch of lay scorn for the medical profession, a remark primly expurgated from the version of the same event written by the good physician Luke (Mk 5:26; Lk 8:43). Note how it is said that the garments of Christ gleamed with a whiteness 'beyond that of any laundryman' (Mk 9:3). The crowds on the lakeside meadowland sat down 'like garden beds' (Mk 6:40; Jn 6:10), for, as John reported years later with that touch of vivid reporting which so often emerged from his strong visual memory, 'there was a lot of grass in the place'.

The list could be extended. In such simple matters, the first raw material of literary criticism is to be found. The truth of a narrative, the authenticity of the writing, must not be predetermined by a fixed attitude toward the miraculous, the unusual, or events beyond immediate understanding.

The second gospel presumes to tell a remarkable story, with all the authority that belongs to a host of contemporary eyewitnesses. Myth does not enter into the question in a contemporary document. Accuracy, reliability, even veracity may be properly examined, but there is no escaping the category of the inquiry; it concerns history, as a man conceived it.

THE DATE OF MARK

Much therefore depends upon the date of Mark's writing. Conservative scholarship reasonably has placed it in the early sixties of the first century. It was an attempt to place beyond danger a record preserved in oral tradition and the poetry of hymns, if the witnesses perished in the coming storm of persecution. That storm was high and dark on the horizon of the church after Nero's sadistic attack on the Roman Christians in the summer of A.D. 64.

It is possible that an earlier date can be claimed, at least for the basic written material Mark incorporated, and that the period of oral and choral retention may be somewhat abbreviated. It is premature at the time of this writing to lay down firm conclusions, but a fragment of papyrus found in 1955 could prove to be a significant piece of evidence for the date of Mark's gospel. This is the story. From Cave 7 in the tangle of hiding places in the cliffs around Qumran on the western coast of the Dead Sea came a set of papyrus fragments in Greek. This was in itself remarkable because few Greek papyrus remnants had come from the other caves, and four caves had yielded no Greek documents at all. All together nineteen fragments were found, but little was done about them until 1962. Only two fragments were identified, one from Exodus and one from the apocryphal Letter of Jeremiah. The unidentified pieces were left in the hands of the Barcelona papyrologist, Father José O'Callaghan, who accepted a dating which made them no older than

A.D. 50 and assumed that he had in hand seventeen pieces of the Greek Septuagint to set beside the two already identified.

Note some basic facts before proceeding further with the story. Cave 7 was one of the Qumran hiding places discovered, not by the local Bedouin, but by competent archaeologists. This meant the find was undoubtedly genuine and had suffered no sort of tampering. The Clarendon Press's third volume of *Discoveries in the Judean Desert of Jordan* came out in 1962 with a plate (No. XXX) showing the fragmentary papyri. Previous to this, a British papyrologist of international repute, C. H. Roberts, had assigned some of the pieces to a pre-Christian date, the piece numbered 5 (7Q5 for future classification) to a date no later than A.D. 50.

Father O'Callaghan, busy preparing a list of papyri for publication, was naturally eager to identify all he could, and since 7Q5 was the largest piece, he began with that. Only ten or a dozen letters from four separate lines were visible, and of them the only possible grouping was the Greek equivalent for *nnes*, which seemed to suggest the word for *generation*. Examination of likely passages from the Septuagint proved baffling, and Father O'Callaghan, his thoughts completely full of the Greek Old Testament, had not considered the New, when a moment of illumination flashed the word *Gennesaret* into his mind.

It did not take him long to find Mark 6:52–53. All the surrounding letters seemed to fit. A mathematician could no doubt calculate the enormous odds against the passage being other than a fragment of Mark's gospel or a written account incorporated word for word in Mark's gospel. The conclusion was checked by colleagues of the discoverer, and by other papyrologists who could not be accused of Christian bias, notably the Yugoslavian papyrologist, Sergio Daris. It took little time, after this lead, to identify the remaining fragments. They were three more minute pieces from Mark (7Q6, 7, 15), a piece from 1 Timothy dated A.D. 100 (7Q4), a piece from James (7Q8), and one from Romans (7Q9) dated respectively A.D. 70 and 60, and a piece from Peter (7Q10) difficult to date.

Criticism of these conclusions there undoubtedly is, for such debates seldom achieve the objectivity of which expert scholarship boasts. Some startling discovery which challenges the whole structure of a corpus of belief is liable, in all but the coolest minds, to stir instinctive hostility. Teachers of ancient history will remember the adjustments made necessary in the study of Hellenic prehistory when the Linear B Script of Crete was deciphered in 1953 and found to be Greek. In biblical studies, the scholar is apt to be emotionally involved, because it is difficult to dissociate literary and historical criticism in that sphere from the articles of faith. There is, in the late John Foster Dulles' phrase, 'agonizing reappraisement'. It is proceeding. It would appear that sustained objection to O'Callaghan's conclusion can only shift the attack to the expertise of two noted papyrologists and the sphere of conflict to the validity of paleographical principles. Discussion over the last two decades seems to favour the conclusion that the fragment was from a written account of the sort to which Luke referred (in chapter 1 of his gospel) and which Mark had in hand.

But consider what it means to have any date from A.D. 50 to A.D. 60 or later. As may readily be seen, if Mark's basic text was in the hands of the church by the middle of the century or soon after, it had to meet the test which any published historical reporting must necessarily face—the critical scrutiny and comment of eyewitnesses: Jews, Christians, Romans, Greeks, who lived in the land at the time of Jesus' ministry. If people thus close to the events, indeed involved in them, found Mark's report accurate, a crucial test of historical writing has been encountered and overcome. And the survival of the account is a sharp presumption that this took place. Christ's first followers must have accepted it as trustworthy history.

It is just possible, then, that a position taken by T. W. Manson could be strengthened. The crisis of A.D. 64 is commonly thought by conservative scholars to have been the occasion for the publishing of Mark's gospel (2 Pe 1:15-16). Manson, in F. F. Bruce's words, 'was willing to push it back into the fifties, considering that a suitable occasion for its publication might have been the reconstitution of the Church in Rome about A.D. 55, after its dispersion when Claudius banished the Roman Jews about A.D. 49'.

Manifestly, firm positions are far from fixed, and the value of the Qumran fragment need not be exaggerated. If it proves of earlier date than A.D. 55, it would add a valuable decade of written testimony to the record. In any case, it remains a fact that, on the basis of existing texts of Mark alone, Jesus is to be regarded as a figure of history, and all assessment and examination of the detail of the narrative must begin at that point.

THE GOSPEL OF MATTHEW

Pass to Matthew. The first gospel, according to Papias, already quoted, had its earliest origin in a collection of sayings of Jesus in Aramaic, which was expanded into the surviving Greek narrative, at an unknown date. The collection of remarkable words and sayings was an ancient practice which can be illustrated in literature from Xenophon to Marcus Aurelius. Several papyri survive which illustrate the practice in a context which concerns our investigation. At the end of the last century, and again in 1904, sheets of such sayings or *logia* were discovered, and more recently, in 1945, the so-called Gospel of Thomas was found by peasants at Naj Hammadi. This was a collection of sayings allegedly collected by Thomas. Some of them are absurd, some could be genuine; they illustrate what could happen to a pure tradition by A.D. 140. The collection also suggests that Jesus' immediate followers collected sayings of their Master. The practice may account for the story of the woman taken in adultery which, though its ring of truth and ancient authority is apparent, may not have been written by John. One remote piece of evidence has been generally overlooked. It comes from the *Chronicles* of De Joinville, the knight who accompanied King Louis on the crusade which set out for Palestine in August 1248. The king thought it wise to appease an ancient sheikh who inhabited the highlands of southern Lebanon and dispatched a brave man, Brother Yves, on this difficult mission.

Brother Yves came back to Acre, and De Joinville reported that 'he found a book by the head of the Old Man's bed, and in that book were written many words that our Lord when on earth had said to Saint Peter. And Brother Yves said to him: 'Ah! for God's sake, sire, read often in this book, for these are very good words.' And the Old Man said he ofttimes did so.'[4] Was this another collection? Was it, perchance, portions of Mark? No one knows, but it helps to establish the tradition of such

practice as that alleged to have formed the original core
of the first gospel.

The marks of such fashioning are clear in the text. The
prominence of the sayings of Christ, including the
Sermon on the Mount, is plain to see. As a bilingual Jew,
the tax-gatherer Matthew was quite capable of expand-
ing an original collection of sayings into the connected
narrative of the book. In its present form, it was known
by the end of the century and was in the hands of
Ignatius, bishop of Antioch, who died about A.D. 107.

The date cannot be precisely fixed, but with the
advent of the imperial persecutions after A.D. 64 and the
darkening shadows over Jewry with the explosion of the
great rebellion of A.D. 66, it may be presumed that the
surviving witnesses of Christ were in some haste to fix
and establish their testimony. These witnesses (themselves, as Pliny's Bithynian letters show, under hostile
scrutiny and suspicion) could not have been in any mood
to make up tales to justify practices and then to die for
such fabrications. The same witnesses were, on the other
hand, under the pressure of considerable urgency to
make sure that a reliable record of those events, for
which they were prepared to suffer, should survive them.
It would, then, seem more appropriate to date
Matthew's gospel before rather than after A.D. 70. The
first gospel again appears as an attempt to write history.
Myth is not apparent. Any account of Matthew's gospel
which disregards the firm tradition of its origin cannot be
regarded as sound literary criticism.

This claim is in no way invalidated by the objection
that Matthew's narrative seems to depend on Mark's in
a manner unlikely in the writing of an apostle and an
eyewitness. Such an objection in no way diminishes the
authority of the document itself. It would indicate no

more than that a second hand was active in the final organization of the document which became the first gospel and quite properly bore the name of Matthew. Nor, in fact, would Matthew's personal authorship and redaction be ruled out. There is every indication of a carefully ordered oral tradition which, in Hebrew fashion (witness the Passover ritual), sought jealously to preserve essential facts and took much note of the form of the words employed. 'I received of the Lord that which I passed on to you' (1 Cor 11:23; 15:1, 3, author's translation) is a clear pointer to this practice. If it is finally proven that the first written records were separated from the events by ten to fifteen years less than was originally thought to be the case, the length of time on which the transmission of an oral tradition depended is, of course, correspondingly abbreviated.

There are also indications in the New Testament of a choral tradition. Hymn-like runs of words and phrases are embedded in more than one epistle (for two examples see Ro 8:31–39 and Phil 2:5–11), and even in early parts of Acts (4:24–30). If the practice is rightly diagnosed, it indicates a determined mnemonic effort to retain uncontaminated a set of essential historical facts and doctrines. Pliny's mention of the morning 'singing of a hymn to Christ or God' may be an example of such credal chanting.

Many considerations could account for Matthew's following an existing narrative by Mark with some care, even to the point of employing Mark's identical words, for it is not impossible that both writers followed an earlier accepted and approved basic account of events. Authority again is in no way diminished; it might even be enhanced. The reasons for such literary phenomena are not always as complicated as remote armchair scholarship, too often in quest of thesis material, is disposed to imagine. The mere act of writing, however pumice-smoothed the face of the great roll of papyrus might be, however well cut the reed pen or well mixed the glue and soot which formed the ink, was a task of considerably more labour than it is today. Nor are the gifts of a ready penman and recorder qualities likely to be found in a man who courted his people's hatred by gathering dues and imposts for a living. He, of all people, might be prompted to adhere to the form of the established tradition. The Lord committed much to some uncultured men. Such men, nonetheless, can witness remarkable events, hear transforming words, and communicate both with utter truthfulness. The same conclusion emerges again: there is no reason to treat Matthew's gospel as other than history, its worth tested by what it contains.

The Gospel of Luke

The third gospel, on the other hand, is the work of a first-rate historian. Luke was a physician, possibly a Greek who had spent time in practice or training both in Antioch of Syria and Philippi. The two traditions of his place of residence could easily both be true. He wrote Greek competently and told a story brilliantly. He claimed, and historical and archaeological research abundantly sustains his claim, to have worked scrupulously, as an historian should, for accuracy. When Paul, upon whom Luke was in attendance, was in the protective custody of the Roman garrison at Caesarea, probably in the years A.D. 58 and 59 (the dates cannot be established with certainty), Luke had a considerable period of unsought leisure in which to scour Palestine for eyewitnesses. Among those eyewitnesses, if the beautiful early chapters of the gospel are to be believed, was Mary the mother of Jesus, now advanced in years.

Luke wrote a second book, the Acts of the Apostles. Any competent investigator will find identity of authorship between the writer of this book and the writer of the third gospel. This second treatise followed the early movements of Christianity insofar as they were preparatory to and connected with the global mission of Paul, up to Paul's time of custody in Rome. The story is largely set in the wider sphere of the Graeco-Roman world and consequently can be tested against the factual background of that world which scholarship has reconstructed from other evidence. Luke passes the exacting test.[5] His gospel, a work of peculiar grace and charm, must have been written along with the Acts of the Apostles or a short time before it. The abrupt ending of Acts suggests that Luke had yet another book in mind, covering the last three or four years of his friend's ministry. He was with Paul in his second imprisonment which was possibly in the year A.D. 67. It follows that his literary activity was before that date. But if ever writing came out of that century which merits treatment as history, it was the writing of Luke.

CONCLUSION

At the risk of labouring the point, let it again be insisted that if any one of the three books which open the New Testament were the only record to survive, that record would need to be approached as history and would constitute by itself a case for the historicity of Jesus. The writers may be dismissed as credulous, mistaken, deluded; but it is impossible to dismiss them as other than real men attempting to set down what they devoutly believed to be true and doing so near the time of the events they reported.

Any other origin for the gospels does not make sense. There exists no possibility of reaching some surviving vein of truth by the strip-mining process called 'demyth ologizing'. The pit deepens, and no ore is found, only lower levels of sterility. Pliny, it may be remembered, discovered through his intelligence agents in Bithynia around A.D. 110, that part of the Christians' dawn religious exercises was a common pledge and under-taking to tell the truth. Some of those who met in Bithynia had heard the apostles in their youth. Some of the renegades confessed to the governor that they had been Christians a generation before. History may be the subject of belief or unbelief; statements in a written record may be set aside as misinformed or untrue but, in the case of the gospels, the records cannot be dismissed as perverse, malicious or fraudulent since those who wrote pledged their lives on the veracity of what they had written.

And what fiction, as that age understood it, can do with the material can be illustrated from the wildly extravagant stories found in the so-called apocryphal gospels of a century later. What happened when the legend-making propensities of later days had room and space to work and spread is illustrated by the gospel of Thomas.[6]

4

The Weaknesses of Demythologization

Demythologization and its weaknesses in literary criticism. The three types of myth and the impossibility of classifying the New Testament under any one of them.

DEMYTHOLOGIZATION

It may be appropriate, at this point in the discussion, to pause and glance forward and backward. We have considered three narratives of Christ's deeds and words and have insisted that these books not only profess to be history, but must be so treated if they are to be understood at all. There is a fourth book in the collection to consider, the gospel of John, which equally purports to be a work of history. However, a lapse of a generation severs it from the synoptic gospels, and that interval is enough, in the opinion of some, to lay it open to the influences which will be discussed in this chapter. It is also somewhat differently conceived as a literary work.

It is, however, necessary to discuss briefly a movement of German origin which has distorted an historical approach to the New Testament narratives as damagingly as did the now discredited theories of the Tübingen school of a century ago.

Since the Christian faith is rooted in history, to disturb the history is inevitably to disturb the faith. Faith proceeds from certain established facts in the historical record—a truth slurred by Karl Barth and carried to absurdity by Rudolf Bultmann. The Tübingen writers produced their critical disasters by gratuitously assuming that a conflict between Jewish and Gentile views of Christianity had determined the form of the New Testament. Bultmann saw the gospels distorted by a 'three-storied' view of the universe. This species of layering of heaven, earth and hell supposedly produced, in a manner not clearly explained, a 'mythical' conception of life, and in the process gave the world the gospels.

Anyone familiar with ancient thought knows that good minds (e.g., Plato and Cicero) were no more preoccupied with this up, down and level notion of existence than is modern man who, in similar unconscious metaphor, thinks simply of this and another dimension of life.* But to proceed, as Bultmann and his followers did, from this oversimplified assumption to a program of 'demythologizing' the story, is not to reach a primitive and recoverable core of truth, nor the person of an 'historic Jesus,' but merely to destroy all evidence and, incidentally, to demonstrate once more that New Testament criticism feels free to follow a path entirely of its own making. In no other department of ancient historical or literary criticism would such a process be accepted as a possible line of fruitful research. It is customary to begin with the documents, their origin, date, authenticity, and so on, proceeding then to their contents. Otherwise the documents will surely be misunderstood.

To extract what is described arbitrarily as 'myth' leaves no residual corpus of information for study. 'Myth,' of

*See, for example, the vividly imaginative *Somnium Scipionis* (The Dream of Scipio) at the end of Cicero's fragmentary *De Republica*. Like the treatise, the concluding fantasy is based on Plato's similar myth.

course, is whatever the critic refuses to accept as possible truth, whatever the evidence, or the authority of the evidence. In his copy of Aristophanes, Rupert Brooke underscored the words, 'The dead do not answer though you call them thrice'—an allusion to an ancient practice of calling the dead three times before the torch was thrust into the funeral pyre. The poet sought, a trifle pathetically, to confirm himself in a chosen stance. Some New Testament critics approach the story of the resurrection of Christ, His deeds of healing, and the circumstances of His birth in the same fashion. 'These things do not happen,' they say, 'therefore they are not true.' But certain documents assert that they *are* true. It proves impossible to discredit the authority of these documents by dating or other legitimate means; therefore sceptical presumptions are found necessary. Hence the invention of the particular type of 'mythology' which is current in this type of criticism.

The term is not one which would be accepted in any other sphere. The classical scholar is immediately aware of some distortion. In the small book of J. B. Phillips which has already been quoted, one catches the instinctive reaction of a man not brought up to think in the jargon of sceptical criticism: 'I have read,' he writes, 'in Greek and Latin, scores of myths, but I did not find the slightest flavour of myth here.'[1]

To set our thinking straight, it will be of some profit to look at three orders of myth which can be usefully distinguished. Each category will be illustrated, and we shall ask if any portion of the New Testament narratives can be placed there. At the same time, the conditions of origin of each form of myth will be examined, and we shall see whether such conditions apply to the emergence or origin of any part of the corpus of material which, to this point in our enquiry, we have put forward as historical. The examination may serve to clear the air of misconception, because before the conclusion of the argument it will be necessary to examine the picture of an extraordinary person set forth by the narrative and to show that this is, in itself, confirmatory information.

THE ETIOLOGICAL MYTH

First look at the etiological myth. This is a story made up to account for an existing situation, fact, or phenomenon. For example, in the hill country of Asia Minor was a town called Lystra. Outside the gate there was a temple to Zeus with two large trees growing before it. The existence of a temple to 'Zeus Outside the Gate' (as one might say 'Saint Martin's in the Fields') is attested archaeologically.[2] Paul and Barnabas had an unpleasant adventure there (Ac 14:6–19), which finds some explanation in a story believed in the district, an etiological myth.

Ovid, that magnificent storyteller, put it into his *Metamorphoses* half a century before the apostle's visit. I shall translate Ovid's skilful hexameters into plain prose.

> Not far from this place is a fen, once a place where people lived but now the watery haunt of marsh fowl. To this place came Zeus, disguised as a man and, with his father Hermes of the Rod, the grandson of Atlas, his wings laid aside. They went to a thousand homes looking for a place to rest, and a thousand homes were locked against them. But one house took them in, only a small one thatched with straw and marsh sedge, but good old Baucis and Philemon of the same age were wed in that cottage in their youth and had grown old together there. They made their poverty easy to bear by not concealing it and enduring it with unruffled spirit. There was no asking for masters or servants there; the two of them were the whole household; together they served and ruled.

So, when the heaven-dwellers came to this humble household and, stooping, entered the low door, the old man set out a bench and bade them rest their limbs, while Baucis busily threw over it a rough rug. Then upon the hearth she pushed aside the warm ashes, stirred to life the fire of yesterday, fed it with leaves and dry bark, and with her aged breath coaxed it into flame. She took down from the roof some fine-split kindling and dry brushwood, broke it small, and put it against the copper pot. From the vegetables which her husband had gathered from the well-watered garden, she lopped the leaves, while he with a forked stock lifted down a smoked side of bacon hanging from a blackened beam. From the long hoarded chine he cut off a small piece and sank it in the boiling water.

Meanwhile they passed the hours in conversation. A long cushion of soft river grass was put upon the couch of willow wood, and on this were put coverlets used only on holiday occasions, poor though these were, a mere match for the willow couch. So the gods were set at table. The old woman, skirts tucked up with trembling hands, put the table in place, and since one of the three legs was uneven, she propped it up with a bit of broken pottery. When this, slipped underneath, had evened the level, she wiped the boards with green mint. She set before them olives, both green and ripe, autumnal cherries pickled in lees of wine, endives, radishes, cream cheese, and eggs lightly cooked in the warm ash, all on earthen dishes. After these dishes, an embossed mixing bowl of the same sort of earthy silver was set before them with cups of beechwood coated on the inside with gleaming yellow wax. Soon the hearth provided its steaming meat, and wine of no great age was produced. Came then dessert: nuts, figs, dried dates, plums, fragrant apples in wide baskets, and purple grapes just gathered from the vines. A comb of white honey stood in the midst. And in addition to all this there were kindly faces and goodwill neither slothful nor poor.

But they saw, as they sat there, that the bowl, as often as it was emptied, kept filling of its own accord. Baucis and Philemon, astonished at the strange sight, fearful and with hands uplifted, begged indulgence for their fare and meagre entertainment. 'We are gods,' said their guests, 'and this wicked neighbourhood shall have the punishment it merits.

But you shall be safe from this evil. Now leave your house and accompany us up the steep hillside.'

They both obeyed, and leaning on their sticks struggled up the long slope. About a bowshot from the top they looked back and saw everything but their own house covered by the waters of a fen. While they wondered at this and wept for their neighbours' fate, that small cottage, small even for its two owners, was turned into a temple; columns replaced the forked supports. The straw turned yellow and revealed a golden roof. There were embossed doors, and the earth became a marble pavement.

Then spoke calmly Saturn's son, 'Good old man, and woman worthy of a man so good, say what you desire.' Consulting briefly with Baucis, Philemon announced their joint desire: 'We ask to be your priest and priestess and to look after your temple, and since we have with one heart lived the years together, let the same hour take us both. Let me never see my wife's tomb, nor be entombed by her.' The prayer was granted. They kept the temple till their life's end. At last, spent with years and age, they chanced to be standing before the shrine and talking of old times, when Baucis saw Philemon, and Philemon Baucis, growing leaves. And as the tree formed over their two human shapes, while cry they could they cried, 'Farewell, dear mate'.

And to this day the peasant points out two trees springing from one trunk and growing side by side. Here ends the myth.[3]

Thus it came about that the Temple of Zeus Outside the Gate had two trees before it; or so the district told, and presumably believed, the story made up to account for visible fact. The peasants of the place, determined this time to recognize the gods, fell to worshipping an unwilling apostle and caused the catastrophe recorded in Luke's narrative. This is an etiological myth. Here is another illustration, one from my own land. Seventy miles south from Auckland, where I live, lies a country township called Ngaruawahia. What does Ngaruawahia mean? An Auckland authority on such matters tells the story, a legend, to be sure, but here it is as it serves our purpose:

> Several hundred years ago the chief of the district was a man named Te Ngaere whose wife was Heke-i-te-rangi, daughter of a chief of the neighbouring Ngati Maniapoto tribe, Uruahu. Uruahu did not favour the alliance, although he had consented to it, believing that Te Ngaere was not his daughter's equal. So Te Ngaere decided to demonstrate to his father-in-law how well endowed he was, how rich his territory was in food, fish, birds and the products of the gardens where the kumara grew on the rich river flats. He invited Uruahu to visit him and made sure that the food storage pits were full to overflowing. These were the 'rua,' those holes in the ground all over New Zealand which tell of former occupation, which intrigue archaeologists and infuriate farmers.
>
> Te Ngaere had a warrior stationed in his watch-tower to give warning of his approaching guests. As the party advanced the warrior called that they were coming. Then he called to his people: 'Nga rua wahia!' And this means: 'Break open the food pits!' So the covers were lifted, and the visitors could see their hosts lifting from the underground stores the wherewithal for a tremendous feast, eels from the river smoked and dried, dried whitebait, birds taken at the right season so that they could be preserved in their own rich fat, kit after bulging kit of kumara and taro, and, no doubt, the freshly gathered vegetable foods of bush and plain and river bank.[4]

Obviously, if one considers these two examples, there is nothing in the New Testament remotely resembling the etiological myth, nothing which mystified another age, demanded some form of explanation, and prompted the inventiveness of storytellers—'the mythopoetic activities of posterity,' if you will have it in the customary jargon. The church demanded no explanation. Even when the century ended and the last books of the New Testament had been written, there were those whose living memory went back to the days of origin. A strong chain of memory can extend for much more than one generation. My own father, to whom I was very close in outlook and in fellowship, was born well over a century ago. He told me of many of his mother's experiences, and she was born in 1833. I knew her when I was a young man, for she lived until 1925. There was no call for invented information about the church, about the apostles, about the Lord. A firm and cherished tradition, carefully embedded in statements and song, answered all major questions long before they became fixed in recorded form. There was no room or occasion for myth or the making of myth.

To suggest that tales like that of the Last Supper were invented to account for a mysterious practice of the church, or that Peter's confession was forged to bolster a doctrine which had inexplicably evolved, is a type of literary criticism which would provoke only a smile in any other sphere of scholarship. The firm and undeniable dating of the records in the first century has cut much hothouse theory at the root. When liberal scholarship could postulate a second-century date for the documents, there was a somewhat wider field for the manoeuvring of fancy. Such open space has disappeared, and with it all late-dating attempts, except for a few desperate efforts to thrust the fourth gospel into the second decade of the second century.

It is clear that there was neither opening nor cause for the production of etiological myth in the New Testament records, and it is as obvious that the second type of myth, the accretion myth, has no foothold either.

The Accretion Myth

The second type of myth may be called the accretion myth, the fiction which, planted and fed by the imaginations of men, grows around some central core of historical truth. The apocryphal gospels, for example, contain a good deal of imaginative material, collected like forest moss around the trees of truth.

The Arthur saga is an example of the accretion myth. It was once assumed that during those years which followed the withdrawal of the Roman regular garrison from the British Isles in A.D. 409, the sea raiders from the North Sea poured in and flooded the land. This was certainly not the case. The province was civilized; it had its militia, and it fought back. It took almost two centuries before the flood of barbarism reached the Severn Valley. Uriconium (now Wroxeter) did not fall to the Saxon invaders till A.D. 582.

One of the leaders of this period of creeping guerrilla war was Artorius, who evidently had great success with cavalry and whose career finished more because of stresses in his entourage than from hostile attack. Nennius, writing near the end of the eighth century, preserved what appears to be a body of historical facts, and there is a tradition of battles in A.D. 518 and 539. Beyond this, history dare not go, but this was the core around which the legendary material about Arthur cohered. As Matthew Arnold said of one of the Welsh contributors, it was sometimes a case of grafting to historical truth 'materials of an older architecture, greater, cunninger, and more majestical'. At other times, the deeds of other heroes, plus the rich imagination of some bard or troubadour, lent their own flavour. So great epics grow. Such poems flourish in societies emerging from a dark age and remembering the deeds of the shadowed years and the persons who lived and battled as an older civilization, half-forgotten, crumbled and fell. Hence the *Iliad*, the *chansons de geste* of France, and other primitive epics which preserve the folk memories of the past and find shape and permanence when civilization resumes after a time of troubles.

An accretion myth thus requires time and usually, in addition, conditions of disturbance, with society feudal and chaotic, writing precariously surviving, and tradition a prey to fancy and confusion. The first century was not such a time. Neither the church nor its Founder contained those materials of romance which could make them the centre of tales of fantasy. The church was a proscribed institution. It had its written records which it cherished. If a few imaginative accounts of the doings of Jesus in His childhood or fabulous events surrounding the resurrection have survived, it was because some were hungry for fiction. The results were probably regarded as fiction, for they won no place among the canonical documents of the church.

Let us repeat and finish the paragraph just quoted from J. B. Phillips.

> I have read, in Greek and Latin, scores of myths, but I did not find the slightest flavour of myth here. There is no hysteria, no careful working for effect, and no attempt at collusion. One sensed again that understatement which we have been taught to think is more British than Oriental. There is an almost childlike candour and simplicity, and. the total effect is tremendous.[5]

THE PLATONIC MYTH

Plato has been properly described as the greatest mind which Europe has produced. His dialogues are one of the finest legacies of Greek civilization. They wrestle, often in the language of Socrates as Plato remembered him or increasingly imagined him, with the age-old problems of ethics and politics, and they are among the most influen-

tial writings of all time. For the purposes of argument
and exposition, Plato developed a type of myth which
was all his own and which has had few imitators. He
would tell a story, admittedly fiction, to suggest a reason
for existing phenomena. Perhaps this is a sophisticated
extension of the etiological myth, but it is different in the
sense that it makes no claim to be true. 'In our myth-
telling,' wrote Plato, 'owing to our not knowing how the
truth stands . . . we make that which is not true serve a
purpose by rendering it as like the truth as possible.'[6]
The myth, in the Platonic sense, must be a good story,
perhaps containing elements of fantasy. It must allay
curiosity and must be obviously unlike history, for it is
not intended to be mistaken for history. Here it parts
company with the etiological myth.

For example, we are all aware of strife and tension in
the depths of our being. This curious duality is something entirely human. One might imagine that in the dim
self-consciousness of a dog or a cat, self is simply the
hunger, the rage, the exhilaration, or the fear which
prompts and feeds the activity of the moment. Men and
women, conscious though they are of the same elemental
urges and desires, can stand back and deny the gratifica-
tion which this 'inner man' craves. On the salutary
exercise of this power, our humanity, our morality, all
our life as social beings, and all our fragile civilization
rests. There are two of us; and one of us, the better man,
must be in control.

The idea is ancient enough. There is not only the New
Testament figure of the 'old man' and the 'new man' at
tension within us, but four centuries before Paul developed his striking image in a letter to the new Christian
community in Rome, Plato told of a conversation with
his master Socrates. To illustrate his point, the great

philosopher concocted the myth about the twin horses of the Charioteer of the Soul. This, says one commentator, was a story built to illustrate 'the disintegrated personality'. The phrase is too extreme for a common experience. Who among men, who hold any sort of ideal, is not conscious of the upward and the downward pull in human nature?

'The charioteer of the human soul,' said Socrates (or Plato speaking under Socrates' name), 'drives a pair, and one of the horses is noble and of noble breed and the other quite the opposite in breed and character. Driving is necessarily difficult and troublesome.' The good horse strives upward, the ignoble horse pulls down, and the task of the good man is to make the base serve the good and drive the chariot upward.[7] There is a wealth of sound psychology here. C. S. Lewis, in *The Great Divorce*, built a similar myth out of his story of the red lizard which, when the angel broke its back, became the stallion on which the emancipated spirit rode at full gallop toward the mountains of light.[8] The dark horse can be tamed and made to serve. And that, in the proper jargon, is 'sublimation' and the 'integration' of the disrupted personality. In such disruption there is no reproach. If one of us is less scrupulous than the other, that person must be made to serve the better and obey. He cannot be killed. That would be to damage life and person. That is what the hermits and the anchorites, running away from themselves into the wilderness and desert, discovered. The old self was still there, loping along with the would-be escapee. He must be befriended, taught to regard the other self, and shown how to serve.

R. L. Stevenson, in his weird fantasy *Dr. Jekyll and Mr. Hyde*, also produced a sort of Platonic myth. Dr. Jekyll made an accidental discovery. He found that a certain drug could isolate his two personalities and allow the lower self to assume a body appropriate to its baseness. The gentle Dr. Jekyll, beloved by all, could become at choice the loathsome Hyde who, uninhibited and unrestrained, could pursue the lust and violence which he desired. The horrible outcome was that Hyde, thus encouraged and fortified, took over, and the change began to take place without any choice and the use of chemicals. That, as every honest one of us knows, is what can happen. There are two of us, as we have said, and one of us must be in firm control.

Those who wish for further illustration could look at the longest and most elaborate of Plato's myths, the story of Er's visit to the underworld at the end of the *Republic*, that great book on righteousness, justice and the ideal state, which ranks high in the list of all the writings of mankind. There Plato builds a fantasy to explain how inequalities of reward and retribution, apparent in this world and so painfully puzzling to anyone who thinks, can be reconciled ultimately with the omnipotence of justice.[9]

But this is sufficient to illustrate the third order of myth, and it is perfectly obvious that the New Testament narratives bear no resemblance whatsoever to the Platonic myth. The writers were not speculative philosophers, any more than they resemble the rhapsodists of the Homeric sagas, or the troubadours or *jongleurs* who, in this part or that of medieval Europe, kept the memory of epic deeds alive in song and renascent poetry. And time, so vitally necessary for the slow concretion of the second type of myth, was altogether lacking.

CONCLUSION

The period which elapsed between the events and their record was brief and set in a civilized world with a high degree of literacy, a world no more ridden by superstition and ignorance than the world of this century. In all essential aspects of life, the world of the first century was more like the world of the twentieth century than was that of any of the intervening eras — city-ridden, prone to the rise of tyrannies, unsatisfied, not a world in which either of the first two orders of myth could find time or place to root and spread.

A perceptive reader might see in John 12:20–36 an allusion by Christ Himself to a myth of a mystery religion based upon the fertility cults. When 'certain Greeks' sought to speak to the Lord, he commented about 'a grain of wheat'.

They could not fail to catch His meaning. A relief from Eleusis in the Archaeological Museum at Athens shows Demeter, the earth mother, presenting Triptolemos, the young prince of Eleusis, with a grain of wheat. Demeter's daughter, Korê, had been abducted by Pluto, god of the nether world; and during her frantic search, Demeter had been entertained by the king of Eleusis. Demeter's anger had so ravaged the earth that Zeus intervened and ordered Pluto to surrender his abducted bride for half of each year—hence winter and summer, the reflection of Demeter's recurrent grief and gladness. In return for Eleusis' kindness, the goddess gave a grain of wheat, which, like Korê, had to go into lower darkness and then return with fruit. Thus came wheat to man.

It was a typical etiological myth, one of the sort alleged to be the origin of the New Testament story of death and resurrection. But surely Christ referred to this to remind the inquiring Greeks that they had symbols of the truth, a sign of rebirth and renewing. The Lord used it prophetically of His own death and resurrection, and the grain of wheat became a mystic symbol in Paul's theology. This is not the climate in which myth itself is created.

The New Testament does not and cannot contain identifiable mythology. The three small Greek books which open the New Testament must be accepted, examined and assessed as history. If what they have to say is rejected, it must be on grounds by which any history would be set aside as false or unproven.

5
Vindicating John's Gospel

John's gospel and the attempts to thrust it into the second century. The vindication of the historical worth of the gospel. The theme of John and its claim to be history. Comparison of style with contemporary writing. The power of memory. The need to classify all four narratives as history.

THE CAMPAIGN AGAINST JOHN'S GOSPEL

The gospel of John, later and differently conceived than the other three, is in a more vulnerable position, which its hostile critics have readily recognized. It was the late W. F. Albright who remarked that Bultmann in particular has carried on 'an unremitting campaign for decades' against this book. It is supposed to contain virtually no original historical matter 'but to reflect an early second-century Christian group tinged more than a little by gnosticism'.[1]

The project of late-dating John's gospel has been pursued with some vigour, for even the gift of twenty years would open attractive revisionist possibilities. If it could be proved that John's gospel was a pious fiction, setting forth what the writer thought Jesus might have said had he lived in the early decades of the second century, then the revisers of Christianity would have a precedent for rewriting the gospels as often as the mood of the moment might suggest and for putting into the lips of Christ whatever sheer romance, narrow prejudice, or special pleading might imagine the Lord to have said in any other age than His own. There is no valid reason for discarding the ancient tradition that the book was written by John, that he wrote his gospel in extreme old age (perhaps in the first half of the last decade of the century which his life almost spanned), and that, since he wrote to refute certain errors in the church, his whole apologetic approach was an appeal to history. His last chapter is striking illustration. He clearly intended to finish his book with the closing words of chapter 20 and then found himself confronted with a nascent legend about his own immortality. Wearily he took up his pen again and refuted the tale which was current. He did so by telling plainly the story of the walk by the lake which had been misreported and misused. The process is the precise opposite of that envisaged by form criticism. A. T. Olmstead, the historian who is quoted effectively by Albright, has maintained that the narratives of John antedate A.D. 40 and represent the very oldest written tradition.

Evidence has made it difficult for liberal criticism to undermine the apostolic authority of the fourth gospel. First, tradition has a proven heavy weight in such matters. The church of the first decades of the second century contained many whose parents and grandparents remembered the apostles, particularly John who was their last survivor. They would certainly not have accepted as genuine the blatant falsehoods of one who pretended to be the revered and well-remembered John, and who untruthfully professed to have stood bravely by the cross and to have run with Peter to the tomb in the garden.

More concrete arguments for the traditional authorship and date are remarkably varied. For the last forty
years some tattered fragments of the New Testament
have lain in the John Ryland's library in Manchester.
They include two broken pieces of John's gospel which
remained unnoticed for fifteen years after their acquisi-
tion in 1920. In 1935 C. H. Roberts recognized their
unique importance. They were pieces of chapter
18:31–33; 37–38, and the handwriting could be dated in
the principate of Trajan or his successor Hadrian.
Trajan died in A.D. 117, Hadrian in A.D. 138. Pick a point
in the middle of Hadrian's principate, say A.D. 126 when
his British garrison was building the wall across northern
Britain. At that time, John's gospel was already well
known and being copied in Egypt. One copy had already
been worn out and discarded. On those two tiny pieces of
brown papyrus much fantasy was wrecked, notably the
old attempt to thrust the fourth gospel deep into the
second century.

They were, of course, not the only piece of archaeological evidence which set John's gospel back in its traditional place inside the life span of John of Galilee. The
recent story of the Bethesda pool (chap. 5) provides
another example. A. Loisy, the French liberal scholar,
suggested that John, or whoever wrote under that name,
had altered the traditional tale to include the five
colonnades. This, of course, was to represent the five
books of the law which Jesus had come to fulfil. Recent
excavations have revealed that before A.D. 70 there
existed a rectangular pool with a colonnade on each of
the four sides and a fifth across the middle. No further
comment is necessary.[2] As late as the thirties of this
century, Loisy was teaching as fact beyond controversy
that the earliest date which could be possibly assigned to

the fourth gospel was at least a decade later than the latest date possible in view of the Rylands papyrus.

Loisy's midcentury date for the fourth gospel was itself a retreat from a more radical position taken by such liberal critics as those of the Tübingen school of the nineteenth century. The discovery of the Gnostic Tatian's *Diatessaron*, the popular harmony of the four gospels compiled near the middle of the second century and containing much of John's gospel, was the rock on which this radical criticism was wrecked. A papyrus fragment from Dura Europos, discovered in 1933 by C. H. Kraeling and consisting of fourteen fragmented lines, reveals first that Tatian's harmony of the gospels was first written in Greek (Syriac and Greek were linguistic competitors), and that it contained John's gospel in the earliest of its versions. The fragment is an account of the request for the body of Christ made by Joseph of Arimathea.

In recent years the discovery of Gnostic documents from Chenoboscion in Egypt has almost rounded off modern knowledge of the Gnostic heresies castigated by the church fathers. It becomes obvious that the gospel of John in no way reflects such thought, whereas there is strong affinity with the language of the Qumran sect. John was using the spiritual vocabulary of an early Judaism rather than a later Gnosticism.

Archaeological confirmation is also available. In the catacombs the raising of Lazarus, a story confined to John (chap. 11), appears in early murals. One in the Capella Graeca of the Priscilla catacomb must be early second century. The vine and the branches form a mural theme in the first-century house of Hermes. An epitaph composed for his own tomb by Abercius, the bishop of Hierapolis who died in the middle of the second century, seems to refer to John 6:68 and the shepherd parables of John 10. W. F. Albright, in the chapter of the book already quoted, devotes two or three packed pages to archaeological confirmation of topographical details, to the nomenclature, and to the term *rabbi*. Ossuary inscriptions verify the names of all the principal characters in the book (including Lazarus as an abbreviation for Eleazer). The 'striking archaeological confirmation of the Greek and Aramaic names preserved in John,' he concludes, 'cannot be accidental'.[3]

THE THEME OF JOHN

The New Testament historians chose incidents and events from the life and passion of the Lord which seemed to them to contain the deepest significance, a choice forced upon any historian. John's whimsical remark at the end of his extra chapter is sufficient comment (Jn 21:25). Strictures on form criticism are not intended to deny the role the gospels played in the practice of the early Christians, nor those influences in their life, discussion and worship which accounted for the survival of some traditions and sayings at the expense of some others. Matters so obvious are taken in the stride of common sense. John, writing with the first movements of a heretical Christology before him, with the teaching of Paul deeply absorbed into the experience of the church, and with some powerful sayings of Christ accepted in an oral tradition and already a familiar part of the common material of evangelism, was naturally selective beyond the synoptists. His purpose, his plan and his methods must be seen within the context of his day and the impact of its needs. He deliberately recovered the imagery of light and darkness from the mystic vocabulary of the contemporary sects, for example those of Qumran. He repeated the thrice told story of the feeding of the multitude (chap. 6) because the sermon on the bread of life flowed from it. He found it unnecessary to carry the same theme on to the breaking of the bread at the Passover table. A simple reading of the book, aided by his first epistle, its covering letter, shows his mind at work.

He told the story of the Pharisee who came by night (chap. 3) and the woman by the midday well (chap. 4), because each were the background for significant and now familiar mystic words. It is possible through the whole book to see the old man working out a plan, and there is no sense of break, literary mutation, or change of style when the story merges into the account of the arrest, the trial, the death and the resurrection of the principal figure.

JOHN'S GOSPEL WAS HISTORY

Whatever his choice of incident, whatever from time to time the reason and motive for the selection, John was consciously writing history in the face of the tensions of the time, seeking to communicate the truth of events significant in his life and doctrine. The whole narrative stands the most crucial test—close examination of detail. For example, note how John's story of the crucifixion contains a gap; certain details are omitted from chapter 19, which can be filled in from the earlier accounts. This hiatus can be shown by careful analysis to mark the time when John was absent, taking Mary home. It resumes with John's return to his place of vigil, a second mile of courage on his part which stirs the heart. Clearly the writer of that fourth account was determined not to include anything which he had not personally witnessed, nothing which he could not say that he had seen.

It was John who told how the rough sponge full of wine was lifted to the sufferer's lips on a spear. The traditional rendering says it was a stick of hyssop. This created a difficulty, for hyssop is a ragged shrub which hangs on walls and is incapable of supplying a rod of any length. It appears that John picked up a dialectical term from one of the soldiers, a term found in both Polybius and Plutarch.[4] Some early copyists, ignorant of the rare term for spear, changed *hussos* into *hussopos*. To be sure, the term *hussos* appears in only one text of the gospel now extant, but the suggestion does make sense of a difficult passage. The word *hussos* was actually the word used for the Roman legionary *pilum* by Plutarch, who wrote a generation later than John. A soldier thrust his spear point into the sponge and held it up. All Peter saw, the spearhead being hidden, was a stick (reed). John reported the facts. These accidental details stamp the mark of authenticity on the narrative.

There are other marks of authenticity: the psychological aptness of the race to the tomb, the conformity to temperament and character of the actions of the two men in the murk of the morning, the unerring placing of the remark about the linen cloth which had swathed Christ's head. In an earlier chapter, Judas opened the door to leave the tense and puzzled group. An oblong of sudden darkness seen for a second stamped itself on one mind forever; and remembering, the writer comments, 'And it was night'. The affidavit following the account of the brutal spear thrust which proved Christ already dead is not to be dismissed any more than solemn, legal affirmations today should be dismissed. Oaths were oaths, reverently made and fearfully regarded.

It is, curiously enough, possible to set beside John's account a letter of Pliny, written at about the same time. We have met Pliny before, and have quoted his letter to Trajan about the Christian problem in his province of Bithynia. Pliny wrote two fascinating letters to his friend Tacitus, in which he describes his personal observation of the great eruption of Vesuvius. In one of the two letters Pliny describes the death of his uncle. His account may be set in illuminating comparison beside John's account of the death of his Friend and Master. If one was history, so was the other. If Pliny sought to report the truth as he knew and remembered it, so did John. And further, if John wrote history, so conceived, when he told of Calvary and death, he wrote similarly when he described the dawn scene in the garden of Joseph and the empty tomb. There is no break in the story, no intruding chapter heading.

Let the methods of history, by all means, be used to test and try the narratives, but let it not be said that the four evangelists were not writing history. Their testimony must be regarded seriously by any student of the past whose task it is to determine whether in Palestine there lived a man called Jesus.

Let us set two paragraphs about a death, one from the Latin of the aristocratic Roman and one from the simple Greek of the old apostle, but written about the same decade, side by side. Pliny was remembering, perhaps twenty years later, the awful August morning in A.D. 79 when the black cloud, like an umbrella pine (we have been taught to speak of 'mushroom clouds') appeared over Vesuvius; and two towns, Herculaneum and Pompeii, disappeared under ash and lava. Pliny was seventeen years old on that summer day and was living at Misenum on the Bay of Naples with his uncle, called in literature 'the Elder Pliny' and mentioned in chapter 1. The old gentleman was in charge of the Roman naval flotilla stationed on the lovely bay, but was also a man of learning and scientific curiosity. Let Pliny tell the tale:

> My uncle, true scientist that he was, deemed the phenomenon important and worth a nearer view. He ordered a light vessel to be got ready and gave me the liberty, if I thought proper, to attend him. I replied I would rather study; and, as it happened, he had himself given me a theme for composition. As he was coming out of the house he received a note from Rectina, the wife of Bassus, who was in the utmost alarm at the imminent danger (his villa stood just below us, and there was no way of escape but by sea); she earnestly entreated him to save her from so deadly a peril. He changed his first design, and what he began out of scientific curiosity, he pursued with high purpose. He ordered galleys to be launched and went himself on board with the intention of assisting not only Rectina, but many others, for the villas stand thick upon that beautiful foreshore. Hastening to the place from whence others were flying, he steered straight for the point of danger, and with such freedom from fear, that he was able to make and dictate his observations upon the successive movements and phases of the dreadful spectacle.

We shall abbreviate, for the present purpose is achieved without quoting the whole of the two fascinating letters. The rescuers crossed to Stabiae, unwisely lingered, and were caught by a new outburst from the mountain. The account continues:

> It was now day everywhere else, but there a deeper darkness prevailed than in the deepest night. They decided to go down to the beach to find out from closer quarters whether they could possibly put out to sea, but they found the surf still running very high. There my uncle, having thrown himself down upon a discarded sail, repeatedly called for, and drank, some cold water; soon after, flames and a smell of sulphur, which was the forerunner of them, dispersed the rest of the company in flight; him they only aroused. He rose to his feet

with the assistance of two slaves, but instantly fell; some
unusually noxious vapour, I conjecture, having obstructed his
breathing and blocked his throat which was not only naturally
weak and constricted, but chronically inflamed. When day
dawned (the third from the last that he saw) his body was
found intact and uninjured, and still fully clothed as in life; its
posture was that of a sleeping, rather than a dead man.[5]

Now look at the contemporary passage from John
(19:16–27, author's translation):

They took Jesus, and carrying His own cross, He went out to
the Place of the Skull, as it is called. There they crucified Him,
and two others with Him, one on each side. And Pilate had a
placard fixed over the cross which read: Jesus of Nazareth, the
King of the Jews. Many of the Jews read it, for the place where
He was crucified was near Jerusalem and the words were in
Hebrew, Latin, and Greek. The high priests of the Jews said to
Pilate, 'Do not put "the King of the Jews" but "He said, I am
the King of the Jews."' Pilate snapped: 'What I have written
stands.' The soldiers, when they had crucified Jesus, took His
clothes and divided them into four parts, one for each of them.
His tunic was left aside. It was seamless, woven in one piece
from top to bottom. They said, 'Do not let us tear this, let us
toss for it.' Thus the text in the Psalms came true, 'They
shared out my clothes, and cast lots for my garment.' This is
exactly what the soldiers did. Meanwhile, by the cross of Jesus
stood His mother with her sister, Mary, wife of Cleopas, and
Mary of Magdala. Jesus saw His mother with the ,disciple
whom He loved standing by her, and said, 'Look, mother,
your son,' and to the disciple, 'Look, your mother'. Straight
away the disciple took Mary to his own home.

But now continue with the same book. In any modern
Bible, the above passage comes from chapter 19, and we
are about to translate chapter 20. In the ancient text
there were no divisions of chapter or verse.

Early on the Sunday morning, Mary of Magdala came to
the tomb while it was still dark. She saw that the stone had
been moved from it, and going to Simon Peter and the other

disciple whom Jesus loved, she said to them, 'They have taken the Lord out of the tomb, and we do not know where they have put Him'. So Peter and the other set out and made their way to the tomb, both running. The other disciple outran Peter, came first to the tomb, and bending down saw the wrappings lying there, but he did not go in. Then Peter arrived, coming up behind him, and he went into the tomb. He looked at the wrappings lying there, and the cloth which had been around His head, not with the other wrappings but folded up by itself in one place. Then the disciple who had reached the tomb first also went in and was convinced.

And there, as the attorney says, the case rests. The three passages are writing of intense vividness. All three must be read, and can only be read, as history.

The Question of Memory

One trifling objection concerning the account of John perhaps needs to be mentioned. It had been suggested that in the aged author memory could play tricks and rob the story of its worth. Any one of us who can look back over half a century knows how wrong is the school song from Harrow which suggests that 'forty years on' we look back and 'forgetfully wonder'. An oral tradition, as anyone who has had anything to do with such a phenomenon knows, can be completely reliable. There is also abundant illustration on record of the power, tenacity and comprehensiveness of the human memory, especially from contexts remote from the props and aids of complex and literate societies. Today we rely too much on paper, tape, film, and are sometimes unaware of the sheer power of the memory.

A curious illustration of this came during the Cook bicentenary celebrations in New Zealand. If the congruent journals of Captain Cook and Joseph Banks for

November 8, 1769 are read, a full account of an incident at Whitianga in Mercury Bay will be found. Lieutenant Gore, to Cook's displeasure, shot a Maori who had stolen a piece of cloth and was making off shoreward from the *Endeavour* in a canoe. It was an unpleasant incident, relieved only by the Maoris' recognition of the thief's folly and fault.

More than eighty years later (eighty, be it noted, not the sixty which lie between the biblical events and John's description of them), an aged Maori, Te Horeta Te Taniwha, lived at Coromandel and reminisced to Lieutenant-Governor Wynyard about the incident. The officer had the story taken down, and the account, some 1500 words, was first printed in White's *Ancient History of the Maori*. The old gentleman told how, as a small boy, he had gone aboard the *Endeavour*. He described 'the chief goblin', Captain James Cook, and spoke of his bearing and authority. He spoke in detail of the theft of cloth and told how Gore went below, produced 'a walking stick,' and pointed it at the canoe which was paddling away. 'Thunder pealed and lightning flashed,' and when the canoe reached the shore 'eight rose to leave the canoe, but the thief sat still with the dogskin mat and the garment of the goblin under his feet. His companions called to him, but he did not answer. One of them went and shook him and the thief fell back into the canoe. Blood was on his clothing and a hole was in his back.'

Note the touch of simple authenticity as the old man put the impressions of childhood into childhood's speech, eighty years after the events. And for all the difference between the language of the old man and the austere and competent prose of Cook and his botanist, the narratives coincide.

UNITY OF THEME

There is no such language gap between John and his fellow evangelists who had written some thirty years earlier. Set Mark's account of the feeding of the five thousand (6:34–46) beside John's (6:5–15). Thirty years, perhaps more, lie between. The details coincide exactly. All four evangelists tell their story with a power born of brevity and intensity of feeling. All four merge their description of Christ in a manner not to be paralleled in ancient history. There are three accounts of Socrates, for example, in Attic Greek literature, from the latter years of the fifth ˉcentury before Christ. Was Socrates, who appears in the dialogues of Plato, an ironical character, passionately sincere, eager for truth, friendly; was he a real man, drawn from life? Or was he, at least in part and increasingly so as Plato's writing continued, a creation of the philosopher's dramatic imagination? This is the problem known as the Socratic Question. Socrates in the dialogues is a clear-cut figure, kindly, keenly humorous, of splendid mental ability. Was he really so conspicuously intellectual? How much of Plato's thought was put into Socrates' mouth? No one can answer. Xenophon, the landed gentleman who served as a soldier of fortune in Persia and wrote a fine description of the retreat of a Greek army from the Euphrates plain through Armenia to the Black Sea,[6] also knew Socrates and left an account of him which is of small historical value. Its genuineness is not known, but Xenophon's Socrates is a fairly homely figure. Then Aristophanes, the comedian and a bitter satirist, put Socrates into a play lampooning the 'new education'. Socrates' whimsical and satyr-like figure lent itself to such caricature, and the young conservative, serious as

was his protest against all sorts of contemporary breakdown, may not have meant to harm Socrates, as in fact
he did.

Observe how three men, as one would have expected
when taking account of their personalities, background,
purpose, and medium of communication, produced three
totally different pictures of the same man. Not so the four
evangelists, quite different though they were in social
context, age, education and personality, and diverse
though the circumstances and the motive of their writing. Their accounts fuse and ring true. Even Ernest
Renan, sceptic in all spheres where the supernatural
intruded, called attention to the manner in which the
words of Christ seem to separate themselves from the
narratives in the four books and shine with a glow of
authenticity. 'A species of brilliance,' wrote Renan, 'at
once mild and terrible, a divine force, if I may so speak,
underlines these words, detaches them from the context,
and renders them easily distinguishable. The person who
undertakes the task of carving out of evangelical history a
consecutive narrative possesses, in this regard, an excel-
lent touchstone. The actual words of Jesus, so to speak,
reveal themselves; as soon as we touch them . . . we feel
them vibrate; they translate themselves spontaneously,
and fit into the narrative naturally.'[7]

FOUR PLAIN STORIES

The four gospels are only small books, written in the
colloquial Greek of the day, one of them in obvious haste,
and yet they agree in portraying One who was not the
product of His times and was far too real and dominant
to be a figment of the imagination. Four men of variant
backgrounds describe a person remote from all their

habits of understanding or the expectations nurtured by their religion. He was One whom they at first clearly failed to comprehend, and only understood at last in transforming reality when an astounding event made both His life and His death significant. This event launched them with such fervour on the world that they infiltrated the great empire in a generation and deflected the course of history.

There is only one ready explanation. Four men, under the dire compulsion of a truth which made them free, wrote of what they saw or of what immediate and reliable eyewitnesses reported to them. It is as Rousseau said, men who could invent such a story would be greater and more astonishing than its central figure.

Like Mark, the first to write the story, John, the last to set it forth, writes plain words which vibrate with truth. I read him often in his simple Greek without translating and always gain an overwhelming impression of his directness, his intimacy with theme and reader. Simply read the story of the wedding at Cana (but correctly rendering, 'Mother, what is that to do with me?') and feel the homely atmosphere, Mary's embarrassment, the best man's feeble joke (chap. 2). Follow on to the story of the rabbi (chap. 3) who came in the night and was annoyed at first because the answer to the question he was not allowed to ask was given by allusion to the books of Ezekiel and Numbers (Eze 36:25–27; Num 21:4–9). And then read the story of the conversation at Sychar's well, with the Samaritan fighting her losing battle of words with the strangest Jew she had ever met (chap. 4). Read on to the poignant account of the Passion Week with its climax in the vivid resurrection stories, paralleled for simple reality only by the narrative in Luke. Simply read. These men were not writing fiction.

This is not what myth sounds like. This is history and only thus set down because it was reporting. These men were writing beyond whatever powers of literary creativity they might have had. Read unpolluted by preoccupation, seeking only truth and not the bolstering of theory; above all read with readiness to accept at any cost that which proves commanding, and seeking no escape.

We add, therefore, the fourth New Testament narrative to the other three and list them all as documents of history. Jesus of Nazareth was a figure of history, and we can know Him as such only as we study the accounts of those who knew Him, and set out, in the grip of a tremendous conviction, to make Him known to the world in which they lived. We shall turn next to consider a matter raised in the last few paragraphs. What kind of a Person was He who moves potently and challengingly out of these pages?

6

The Personality of Jesus

The extraordinary nature of the Person described in the gospels, and the impossibility that such a character could have been invented. His humanity and His distinctions from humanity. His universality.

THE STILL LIVING PAGE

Consider now the point to which the argument has led us. Jesus, beyond all doubt, is a figure of history. That fact is confirmed by evidence outside the Bible. In the light of this evidence, the gospels take their place as authentication. The position has also been taken that, quite apart from secular evidence, the four New Testament narratives could stand alone as confirmation of the presence and activity in Palestine of an extraordinary man, whose followers and their convictions about Him changed the whole course of history.

An extraordinary man—so extraordinary, in fact, that here, perhaps, is found the taproot for the scepticism which infects New Testament studies and occasions the curious inhibition of which we have more than once complained, the seeming inability to treat the New Testament documents as the stuff of history, and to approach them only with those preconceptions and prejudices which corrupt all argument.

A sad word was once said by Jesus Christ. 'I came,' He said, 'not to send peace, but a sword' (Mt 10:34).

Mankind divided around Him. His challenge precipi-
tated crisis and choice. 'He is the anointed of God,' said
some. 'No,' said others, 'He deceives the people'. The
schism extends to those who read the story. Inevitably
He involves the reader, but does not a cogent argument
for His reality appear at precisely that point? Does not a
personality different from all mankind so stand out from
the pages of the gospels, that He is beyond invention and
must be real? And are not the miracles, which baffle the
modern mind, of small account before the miracle of a
unique character?

No person through the nineteen centuries which have
known His story has stirred such intense love, loyalty
and devotion. In poetry and prose, in mighty works of
art, in music, and in all manner of beneficent and
sacrificial activity, Jesus Christ, known only through His
witnesses, has filled the thoughts of men. Plato writes of
Socrates with greater elegance than the evangelists wrote
of Christ. The story of Socrates' death, ironical to the
end, can stir the heart and fill the mind, but close the
book and life resumes, uninvolved, unchanged. Not so
with the story of the cross.

A typical reaction was a few years ago in print.[1] It was
a testimony from John Lawrence, classicist, linguist,
diplomat and journalist. The contributors to a symposium spoke of their belief in God, and Lawrence told
how, bemused by university philosophy—that most
corrosive of disciplines, one is bound to say, in too many
academic contexts—he had found a clear childhood faith
grow dim and how he rediscovered his belief by way of
the New Testament. He wrote:

> The vague but vivid beliefs with which I started were slowly
> worn away over more than twenty years. I went to church less
> and less often. . . . I never said my prayers. Perhaps I should

have settled for the grey world that was slowly opening before me, if I could have forgotten my childhood's vision of splendour. But when the last glow had faded from the horizon, the world seemed inexpressibly cold and dreary. I was acutely unhappy. . . . Then I considered the fact that, if nothing was proved, equally nothing was disproved. . . . Ought I not to look again at Christian belief? So I got out my Greek Testament and began to read Mark's Gospel, a few verses a day. When I was about half way through I began to ask myself, 'Who then was Jesus? Was He more than a man?' After that I was over the top of the hill.

The writer had taken the book as a document of history as any trained classicist would. Uncommitted at first as to its truth, he encountered the person of Jesus and asked himself the obvious question.

The Person of Jesus

Mark's account of how it all began has an advantage, because it plunges the reader headlong into the midst of the desert revival led by the fiery Elijah-like figure of John the Baptist. The strangely beautiful and reserved stories of the nativity and the flash of light on a gracious childhood with which Luke opens his narrative might have daunted a sceptical and disillusioned mind. To turn back these pages after an encounter with the mature Christ is to find their wonder merge with the total picture without incongruity. Those who knew Him found it no strange and incredible story when Mary told them of the nature of His coming. She was not dismissed as a liar or a charlatan. The first shock and amazement passed after that tremendous Passion Week, His men found nothing incongruous in His victory over death. In the conviction that they had seen the risen Christ, they flung themselves on the evil world and snatched trophies of life from its decaying fabric, as such trophies are snatched still today in every land.

Jesus moved into the disturbed scene of a nation's soul searching and religious revival with quiet authority. John the Baptizer, no pliant and self-effacing person, suddenly overwhelmed by the fact that he had failed to recognize the One he had come to proclaim, bowed in reverence before Him as though conscious of much which the brevity of the account has kept from our knowledge. John's conviction must have been so obvious, and so clearly congruous with what they saw that his own followers turned from their passionate master and followed an altogether different man.

It seems clear that during the youth and early years of Jesus the hillside town of Nazareth, with that illogical obtusity which has denied many a good man a reputation among his own neighbours, saw in Jesus only the son of the carpenter and the brother of young men and women whom they knew. In the days of His ministry, He found Himself restrained and inhibited by their refusal to see the movement of the divine in Him. He could do no great work among them because of their unbelief (Mk 6:5–6). He was thirty years old before the days of testing in the grim Judean wilderness above Jericho, when the manner of His ministry was before Him, the subtle urge to wonder-working, the strong temptation to take the short path of popular appeal, a more earthly road to eminence.

The picture builds rapidly, and any first-time reader of Mark's account would find himself turning the pages to discover whether the other writers would in any way explain the remarkable phenomenon taking sharp and unique shape, as the simple sentences run on. The figure of Jesus is obviously commanding. The scribes and rabbis were revered persons in the land, feared for their sanctity and admired for their meticulous observance of the Law, but here was One who spoke with greater authority than they, yet who had no seal of rigorous education, who handled the Law as if He had a right to revise and to reinterpret it, and yet in such a manner that none who heard Him could quote this word or that to point a charge of blasphemy against Him. And the curious fact becomes apparent, as the reader moves on, that here was a person who had no consciousness of sin, and yet was accounted good. It is the sure mark of every other good man that a deep consciousness of unworthiness and weakness underlies his piety; witness Isaiah, Peter, Paul. Repentance for wrong-doing and moral inadequacy is the invariable beginning of all human goodness, and the noblest men are those most conscious of their human imperfections. Yet Christ, whose very presence stirs the consciousness of unworthiness in others, never Himself repents, never seems to regret word, thought, or deed, betrays no passing shadow or sense of wrong, inadequacy, or failure. He confidently claims to have lived a life that glorifies God Himself. With the stern and hostile faces of those who sought His life ringed around Him He could ask: 'Which of you can point to sin in Me?' None picked up the challenge in exultation, none dared to speak and say that such a question in itself was a piece of arrogant self-righteousness, which marked the fundamental of all sins—a damning pride. In Him it did not seem arrogant. Nor can the words be expurgated from the text by some process of revision. They are not likely to be the stuff of invention.

In other words, Christ deliberately distinguishes His piety from ours. No mere man could adopt this attitude and maintain it. If the stance did not itself call down derision, the one making so audacious a claim would soon himself be betrayed into delinquencies which would turn his closest friends away. If one harbours passion unchecked by a humbling consciousness of weakness, pride checked by no spirit of repentance, self-righteousness without cleansing introspection, how long would it be before all these would issue in acts of patent sin? In Him no debacle follows. He begins with a nonpenitent piety, and He successfully maintains it. Either we have here a perfect being or we have in Him a piety that denies all the laws of nature, for, though it is wholly unsuited to the character of any man, it has won the world's respect. We have recorded in the gospels a character which defies all the laws of normal psychology. It is impossible that this character could have been human, in the word's common significance. This is what occasioned the vital question asked by John Lawrence in the quotation at the beginning of this chapter.

REVERSAL OF HUMAN EXPERIENCE

Nor let it be forgotten that He was under the most rigorous scrutiny. It was no passing hysteria which gave Jesus His reputation, no gust of collective enthusiasm which swept Him to leadership and found comfort and justification in the delusions which have driven men to wild loyalties. They knew Him, those shrewd and intelligent men, and knew Him well under the most exacting circumstances. The outcome was that He grew more sacred to them.

Familiarity may not always breed contempt, but in all of our normal human relationships, it reveals eventually our weaknesses and blemishes. All our human friendships must be based on the give and take of mutual indulgence. One of the sources of youth's disillusionment is the fading halo around the head of some human hero it has hastily sought to worship. Not so with Christ and His disciples. For three years they trod together the lanes and byways of Galilee and Judea. They climbed together the rough roads up to Jerusalem, sat together in the lush grass above Tabgha. Together they bore the heat of Jericho and the cold winds of the Galilean lake. They shared His chill rest beneath the stars, His breakfast on the beach. Together they bore the storms and tensions in the holy city, together they enjoyed Bethany's hospitable home. Surely this was test enough if shrewd men were to know Him. What happened? Far from detecting the hidden flaw, the human burst of annoyance at the end of a weary day, personal ambition betrayed by a chance word or unwise confidence, far from finding in Him disappointing blemishes, they found that their sense of wonder and reverence grew.

Familiarity only seemed to make Him a deeper mystery. This was as true for His friends as it was true for His enemies. Peter, so ready to blurt out his inmost thoughts, seems to become more silent as the days go by. At the supper the once bold disciple beckons to his younger friend to whisper and ask who the betrayer might be, and later the same night, as he stood distraught by the brazier in the courtyard of the high priest's house, one glance from Christ breaks and shatters him in anguish. What of His enemies? First He is but some new fanatic; 'no prophet comes from Galilee' (Jn 7:52). He soon commands their attention. His intellectual and moral accomplishments excite wonder, and the proud priestly caste turn all their wit and power to the task of tripping Him in His words and discrediting Him before the people. They try to arrest Him, but the officers shirk the task. The excuse? Merely that 'Never man spake like this man.' The party who effects the arrest in the garden on the betrayal night are in such terror of apprehension that His very glance will blast them, that at His first word they reel back in confusion. This was no supernatural visitation. He was simply by the power of His presence in command of the situation. Pilate, caught in the net the clever priests had spread for him, was so shaken by the deed he was forced to do that he took water and washed his hands before them in anxious symbolism. He desperately needed to be clean. What manner of Man was this?

CONTRARY TO ALL EXPECTATION

Consider how impossible it would have been for the writers of the gospels, whoever they might have been and whenever they might have written, to create out of aspiration and imagination the character which confronts the reader of the gospels. Consider how equally impossible it would have been, after such close association and fellowship, to imagine and graft into their story details not obviously known and observed.

The Jews had a clear image of their expected Messiah. His coming was part of popular belief. The woman at the Sychar well spoke of the Messiah from whom all final answers would come. A fisherman declared to his amazed brother that he had found the expected one. The crowd, talking in the city street, measured the person of the Prophet from Galilee against their popular expectations of what the Messiah should be. However, those who followed Christ soon found that He did not fulfil their preconceived notions. This may have been a factor in Judas' desperate decision to betray Him. But in spite of the way He bewildered and frustrated them, He held the rest to their loyalty, almost—at times—in spite of their prejudices.

He seemed to care nothing for the bitter humiliation of their land. He told His cunning critics to pay back to Caesar the silver denarii they had accepted at Caesar's hand. When a brilliant rabbi came in puzzled curiosity to ask when Israel's kingdom would be restored, He told him to think rather of another kingdom, which only those whose lives are transformed will gain, and played felicitously on the man's knowledge of Ezekiel to make His meaning clear.

'I am meek,' He said, 'and lowly of heart' (Mt 11:29). That was obvious in His whole demeanour, and yet He claimed that Moses had written of Him, that Abraham had looked forward to His day; He claimed to be greater than Solomon, and of deeper significance than the revered temple of God. He spoke of oneness with God and a Sonship beyond their comprehension. In simple words He asserts that He is the penitent's way to God, the end of philosophy's quest, the goal of a dying world's desire, in His phrase, 'the way, the truth and the life'. As if all light, all wisdom lived in Him, and assuming every right to do so, He opened His arms to burdened mankind and 'Come,' He cried, 'all ye that labour and are heavy laden, and I will give you rest' (Mt 11:28). Yet of those who so came He demanded an abandonment of love which only God has the right to claim; and allegiance which overrode all earthly affection, all regard for self or kindred. With no sense of incongruity, but with all the anguish of pure rejected love, He wept over Jerusalem, hard and priest-ridden, the persecutor of prophets. How often would He have 'gathered her penitents together, as a mother bird her brood' (Mt 23:37). If this were merely a man speaking, was there ever effrontery so preposterous?

All these claims, these strange exotic words which Renan found so revealing, are woven quite inextricably with the record. Some have undertaken without success to strip them away and discover 'the historical Jesus'. It has proved impossible to do so. The historical Jesus is the being who claimed what no other man has claimed, and who yet, such was the authority inherent in Him, has not been considered mad, bad, or in any way less than the best of mankind. It is obvious that for true seekers after truth, the basic question is the one which forms our title and which the seeker we have quoted asked and found himself immediately across the summit of his life's inquiry. *Who was Jesus?* The truth of Christianity stands or falls with the Person of its Founder. The wonders claimed for His birth, and His triumph over death, fall naturally into place if He was more than man.

A SINGLE FIGURE

How curiously the force of that personality and His words which so cogently give it expression, extend themselves down the ages and find respect for their remotest echoes. I have quoted elsewhere the best known of modern historians, Arnold J. Toynbee.[2] Make what you will of the amazing scholar's allusive style, his testimony to Christ's worth and to the potent projection of His claims down the long corridor of history remains. Halfway through the sixth volume of his *Study of History*, Toynbee makes a remarkable comment. He has discussed for some eighty pages the 'saviours of society,' those who by defending the past, by reaching for the future, by war or peace, by power or persuasion, by claims to wisdom or claims to divinity, have sought to stay some social catastrophe, some disintegration of a culture. Toynbee concludes:

> When we first set out on this quest we found ourselves moving in the midst of a mighty marching host; but as we have pressed forward on our way, the marchers, company by company, have been falling out of the race. The first to fail were the swordsmen, the next the archaists, the next the futurists, the next the philosophers, until at length there were no more human competitors left in the running. In the last stage of all, our motley host of would-be saviours, human and divine, has dwindled to a single company of none but gods; and now the strain has been testing the staying-power of these last remaining runners, notwithstanding their superhuman strength. At the final ordeal of death, few, even of these would-be saviour-gods, have dared to put their title to the test by plunging into the icy river. And now as we stand and gaze with our eyes fixed upon the farther shore, a single figure rises from the flood, and straightway fills the whole horizon. There is the Saviour; 'and the pleasure of the Lord shall prosper in his hand; he shall see of the travail of his soul and shall be satisfied.'[3]

A single Figure rises.

There is simple tribute to that unique personality in the eagerness—appropriate and inappropriate—of a thousand groups to claim Jesus for their own. Rebels and fugitives from any sort of established society lay hold of Him as patron saint. Marxist, Communist, revolutionary and protester profess to interpret Him. But leave such eccentricities aside as a curious demonstration of the fascination His Person can thrust into the most unlikely corners of time and of society—leave aside the pathetic desire of the remotest alien to reach out for Him—and some other features of tremendous significance remain.

REAL HUMANITY

The first is that all the extraordinary claims which mark His difference are found in a person of intense and real humanity. J. B. Phillips, in the remarkable little book we have had occasion to quote, speaks of his own experience with Christ, as he read the Greek Testament intensively as he made his new translation:

> What happened to me as I progressed (he said), was that the figure of Jesus emerged more and more clearly, and in a way unexpectedly. Of course, I had a deep respect, indeed a great reverence for the conventional Jesus Christ whom the Church worshipped. But I was not at all prepared for the *unconventional* man revealed in these terse Gospels: this was no puppet-hero built out of the imaginations of adoring followers. This man Jesus, so briefly described, rang true, sometimes alarmingly true. I began to see why the religious Establishment of those days wanted to get rid of him at all costs. He was sudden death to pride, pomposity and pretence.[+]

In fact, schooling the mind to do so, one could turn back to the beginning of the gospels, having been daunted by His uniquely divine qualities and discover in a second reading Jesus the man: one could almost see Him pick a flower on the mount of the Beatitudes, look closely at its wide-petalled loveliness, and compare the fragile thing to Solomon, robed and spangled. He looked a murderous mob in the eyes and walked calmly through the lane the ruffians made for Him. He went north to rest and found so much work to do that He grew exhausted coping with it. He slept in a lurching boat as the storm wind funnelled down the Jordan rift and the fishermen toiled at the rowing. He wandered away to pray and bade the disciples begone. They went. He sent them off to buy provisions and wearily sat on a well, conversing with a woman who at first sought to irritate and annoy

Him. He clearly needed to be alone at times, and His men had to learn to read the signs on His face. They at times failed to read His loneliness. As He strode ahead on the Jerusalem road, the small party lagged behind and bickered, finally breaking into His sad preoccupation with a mad request. He answered in quiet and disappointed weariness.

He could communicate with the outcast, the rejected, and calm the wildly insane. He wept in the presence of shattering human sorrow. With the great, hard, tradition-ridden city before Him, He wept again over mankind's collective rejection and a nation's blindness to the offer of peace, as though He saw the Roman earthworks rising and the ballistas hurling their whistling stones. To follow the old lanes in Jerusalem, in the traditional stations of the cross, is to catch the sense of His humanity with almost unbearable poignancy, the stumbling under the load, the word to the sorrowing women.

He could say terrifying words about hypocrites, about the merciless, about those who harmed children. He could forgive with disconcerting ease. He could accept hospitality. He wore good clothes (the cloak woven without seam was no beggar's garment). How can the gospels be read with these two distinct preoccupations—to encounter a God-man, and to meet a man tempted and tried in all points like one of us? Surely it can only be because men knew a man like that and experienced this dual fellowship with such intensity that truth broke full featured and full length into the written testimony.

UNIVERSALITY OF CHRIST

Second, consider the universality and living vigour of His words, relevant, applicable if ever words deserved such adjectives. They rise out of the ancient text, invade other centuries, carry their continuing conviction. They should seem quaint, out of touch, but they do not. They should seem impracticable, but are not: every age has seen men and women of every nation put them success-fully to the test. They should seem remote from common life, but they are not: all time has seen multitudes find in Christ a centre for ordinary living, a light for common day. They should seem alien, ancient, Jewish, but they are not: Christ is universal as is no other person in all history.

A statue of Winston Churchill in his home village of Westerham shows him rugged and strong, gazing down the Weald. He could only be an Englishman of his time and class. Not so Christ. Natural and complete though He seemed within Himself, His age did not produce Him as the disillusioned lethargy of India produced the Buddha, the dry wisdom of China Confucius, and sol-dierly Iran its enduring Mithras. Neither Greek, Roman, nor Jew shaped Christ. And yet all races have had their hosts who have accepted Him and found Him theirs. He belongs strangely to mankind. A German painter shows the walk to Emmaus in a Rhineland setting. The three robed figures move among summer elms; a village church is in the distance. In the stained glass windows of a church in 58th Street, New York, the same scene is set in New England. In the Maori Church at Ohinemutu, among the hot pools on Lake Rotorua's edge in New Zealand, a Maori Christ in a rangatira's robe is etched in such a way on a plate glass window, that from the pews He appears to walk on the water. It is an admirable conception, especially where the far shore looks oddly like the coast of Galilee. He does walk on New Zealand's lake. All nations have received Him whole.

This universality is a strangely significant fact, because it is obvious that if Jesus were the creation of the imagination, He would bear the marks of His time and place upon Him. We have seen that He frustrated the Messianic expectations of His own people, even His own disciples, and yet held their love in spite of all. No Jew inventing a new Messiah would have invested a figure of fiction with characteristics so alien.

Across Galilee and east of Jordan were the ten towns of the Decapolis. Probably hundreds of thousands of Greeks lived there, populations perhaps not unlike that of cosmopolitan Corinth—sophisticated, aware of philosophy but abusing it in the same way that stirs Paul's quiet irony in the first four chapters of 1 Corinthians. There is no evidence that the expatriate Greeks of Palestine had much influence on metropolitan Jewry, but had they done so their ideals could not have created the figure of the gospels. He was in no way the philosophical ideal of Stoic or Epicurean: unmoved, withdrawn, aloof, garrisoned in mind against life. He was alone, different, yet universal, related to all. Could there have been a stranger paradox?

The One described in the gospels bears His own authentication. There is no way past the contention that Jesus lived according to the proportions measured in the story. It is against this background that His claims and what the New Testament claims for Him must be assessed.

FOOTNOTE

Professor Purushotman M. Krishna, writing of the appeal of Christ, has some interesting words to say. This outstanding scholar is a convert from Hinduism. His

words are relevant because, as C. S. Lewis once perceptively remarked, the only competitor against Christianity
for the souls of men is the Indo-Aryan world view
(Hinduism and Buddhism with their various derivatives
and interpretations). Professor Krishna sees the only
answer to such rival cults in the historic Christ. (This
was the secret of the victory of Christianity over
Mithraism in its early centuries.) Christ, he says, must
be 'lifted up'. Lifting up Christ in this context simply
means presenting the claims of the historical Jesus in
three indisputable areas. First there is:

> (The) whole aspect of his life where his moral impeccability,
> his majesty, and his perfection shine out like a beacon light for
> all to see. There is no room for argument here—the moral
> grandeur of Christ silences any dissent. Consider him when he
> was here on the good earth as an incarnate man. Examine him
> closely—his obedience to God's commands, his compassion,
> his instant sensitivity to the needs of others, his approach-
> ability. He must have been indeed the most approachable man
> of all time. Sinners and publicans thronged him even when he
> sat to eat; they even tore down a roof to get to him, without
> being reproved. Look at the portrait of him dealing with that
> tense situation in which a woman taken in adultery was
> perilously near to being stoned to death, and his gentle
> deliverance of her. Or look at his reaction to his enemies and
> all the calumnies and pain they inflicted upon him. On one
> occasion, against strong pressure, he flung a challenge at the
> feet of his detractors—'Which of you convicteth me of sin?'
> (John 8:46)—and no one dared to respond! His moral purity
> was too patent and glorious for even his enemies to deny.[5]

The second and third areas are the teaching and
resurrection of Christ, but it was Professor Krishna's first
point which made, coming from such a man, so striking a
footnote to the theme of this chapter.

7
Examining Alleged Faults in Christ

An examination of aspects of the stories in which the character of Christ has been alleged to be faulty. The Cana wedding. The incident of Martha and Mary. The Syro-Phoenician woman. The cleansing of the temple. Anger. Brusqueness. Rejection of the term 'good'. 'Man of sorrows.' Temptation. Rejection at Nazareth.

RABBI OF TARSUS

There is no doubt at all that the truth of Christianity (and how urgent is that truth for the whole future of man!) stands or falls with the validity of the tremendous claims of its Founder. If He was not God's last word to man, His ultimate revelation of Himself, divine in a sense in which no other religious leader has ever claimed divinity, if, in short, Jesus sought to deceive or was grossly mistaken about Himself, Christianity is a delusion which has distorted almost twenty centuries of history. Nothing of the most universal of religions remains if Christ was deceived, mad, or misrepresented. And those who have committed life and person to an error so tragic are, in the words of an early and extraordinary convert, 'of all men most miserable'.

The writer of that uncompromising statement is worth a glance. He was Paul, the learned rabbi of the Cilician city of Tarsus, an educated Hellenist, a Roman citizen by right of birth, one of the most intelligent men of his century. He knew the authors of the books which have been our preoccupation. No doubt it was under his active encouragement that his friend and associate, Luke, had scoured Palestine for further facts. He had himself experienced the compulsion of those facts and had resisted their impact until he was at last overwhelmed by them.

It was not long after the midpoint of the century, ten or twelve years before Mark wrote his brief account of Christ, that Paul wrote a letter to the Christians of a church he had founded in the cosmopolitan port of Corinth. He had arrived there determined to be simple, to cut through the clutter of all the town's philosophic pretensions, and press home the essentials of his convictions.[1] He knew the price he had paid for those convictions—honoured standing with his peers, privilege of caste, liberty. He was no pursuer of lost causes.

At that time he stood nearer the vital events of Christ's ministry than the writing of this chapter stands to the end of the Second World War and the stormy beginnings of the Lost Peace. He could feel the power of the living Christ, in the earthly sense of that word. True enough, that power still moves heart and mind; but when Paul wrote to Corinth, it was fresh in memory. It was the tradition built of that memory which he had passed on to the Christian congregations multiplying in the eastern Mediterranean, and indeed as far as Italy. It was strong and clear, and it was woven, as we have seen, with lyrics of worship, still distinguishable in the text of the New Testament—a fact of deepest significance, because those who encountered Jesus found it impossible to dissociate events from the question of His authority and the nature of His person. The letter to Corinth shows that Jesus was accepted as utterly unique, the conqueror of man's last enemy, the promised Saviour: that which Christianity has always held to be true of Him was held and insistently preached even before the gospels were written.

THE GOSPELS AND THE TRADITION

The oral tradition which was the material of the earliest Christian preaching, the link between the events of the life and death of the Lord and the preaching of the evangel, was a body of vital events, significant sayings, and credal statements. And apart from the intriguing papyrological evidence of an early text of Mark, it is more than likely that memoirs, credal statements, stories, and the texts of hymns like the one the Bithynian Christians sang, 'to Christ as God' must have circulated. Luke mentions that many sought to set down a record of events. We have noted the existence of collections of sayings. When, therefore, the New Testament narratives became current, many Christians throughout the empire must have become aware of words and incidents which widely expanded their knowledge of Jesus, the historic person. This was especially true of the fourth book in which John added several incidents because they provided background and context for sayings which he thought important to his theme. We have already noted that some responsible opinion would date the stories in John's gospel as part of the oldest written material in circulation.

These additions, commonly told with an objective simplicity which is itself a demonstration of honest reporting, are often the portions of the record which have provided material for some who have sought to diminish the Christian concept of the historic Jesus. But note that the early church appears to have found no contradiction between the picture of Christ that became current with the multiplication of the gospels in the Greek-reading world and the Person who had been presented and accepted as the central theme of an evangel that went back in a short chain of unbroken links to the apostles and their proclamation.

The first readers of the written gospels were, in fact, in a specially favoured position to assess the historical value of what they read. There are incidents recorded, and facets of Christ's character and person revealed, on which we might be glad to have greater information or more background material. In many cases, the early Christians were in possession of those exegetical advantages. They knew the surrounding circumstances of material or report on which hostile criticism has fastened. They were not, for example, aware of marks of faulty character calculated to mar that image of perfection which stirred the love and reverence of those first associated with Jesus.

It must be remembered that the ancient world wrote with great brevity, due to the sheer physical difficulties of writing, the limitations of a roll of papyrus, and the greater reliance upon oral communication. When John, for example, wrote in Ephesus the story of the cleansing of the temple, he was aged, to be sure, but in full possession of his faculties and available to supply details which set the incident in context and perspective. When Matthew included in the final draft of his book the stern denunciation of the Pharisees, he was able to fill out the narrative in person.

It remains for us honestly to do the same. In conclusion we shall return to the historical documents, which, we have insisted, reveal a Person quite unique among men, and ask frankly whether we have followed a Christian tradition which is not based on all the evidence the narratives offer, but one which makes up its picture of moral perfection by a process of selection. Was Jesus indeed, as Kierkegaard put it, 'the paradox which history can never assimilate,' or was He a man like any other man, sometimes ungracious, given to anger, even violent? These faults have been alleged, and it is necessary to look at them in turn asking whether the few who, in human fashion, have sought to reduce Him to human proportions have any foundation for their argument.

WEDDING AT CANA

Turn first to the second chapter of John and that seemingly ungracious remark of Jesus to His mother. Christ, His mother and His disciples were invited to a wedding in the Galilean village of Cana, just over the hill from Nazareth. Hospitality, largely daring, had overreached itself, and the wine gave out. Mary, agitated over the social disaster to friends, came to her Son. 'They have no wine,' she whispered. The translators, strictly following the lexicon, render His reply, 'Woman, what have I to do with thee? My hour has not yet come.' No amount of theological explanation can remove from those words the sting of rebuke and the bitter flavour of unfilial harshness. Hence the dilemma, for all such harshness was completely alien to Jesus Christ. The translators might have realized that something was wrong. Words out of character are likely to be incorrectly rendered. Such is undoubtedly the case here.

It has come about in English that the generic term *woman* is a rude mode of address. Chivalry invented more polished terms for womankind. That is not the case with Greek. The sixth book of the *Iliad* illustrates this. That portion of Homer's mighty poem on the tragedy of Troy contains one of the most tender passages in all ancient literature. On the walls of Troy, above the embattled hosts, Hector, bravest of the brave, says goodbye to his wife, Andromache, before going out to fight yet again. The sense of doom is over Andromache, and she implores her husband to venture less in the forefront of the strife. In a noble speech Hector replies using the very Greek word of John's story, *woman*. S. O. Andrew translates it *dear wife*, Cazley *dear lady*, and Leaf *my wife*. Andrew's translation begins:

> That is my concern, dear wife: I were strangely ashamed,
> The Trojans to meet and their wives in their trailing robes,
> If here like a coward I skulked aloof.[2]

Why the translators of the New Testament, on like principles, could not have rendered the word in the Cana story as 'dear mother' or 'lady,' is a mystery. I note that the two Italian translations which I possess render the word *Donna 'Lady,'* which is a good translation. *Madonna* is 'My lady' herself!

But what about the actual remark? It is true that if a Jew wished to brush a nuisance off or brusquely to repel an advance, he said, 'What to you and to me?' So the phrase runs quite literally. It means, 'What is there in common to you and me; what contact have we between us?' The maniac of Gadara uses the phrase, 'What to you and me, Thou Son of God?' and the translators correctly render, 'What have I to do with you?' It is also true that in the Greek translation of Christ's words in the Cana story this formula is used. But Christ spoke in Aramaic; in the Greek New Testament, we are already one language removed from the original. I am convinced He said, 'What is that to you and Me?', a perfectly natural remark when a fellow guest notes a host's embarrassment and asks another guest to intervene without formal invitation to do so. The words took the form in the Greek of the common idiom of dismissal and have been misunderstood ever since. I have looked at twenty-seven translations in English, two in French, two in Italian, one in German, one in modern Greek, and one in Hebrew. All but two perpetuate the mistake. Only Phillips and C. M. Lamsa render it correctly. 'Is that your concern or mine?' says the former, and Lamsa, 'What is it to you and to me?'

See how the story falls into place now. 'They have no wine,' Mary whispers. 'Nothing to do with us, Mother dear. My hour has not yet come.' (i.e., 'This is not My feast.' When He did provide a feast, nothing lacked.) Knowing Him, and after the fashion of mothers leaving no time for refusal, she turns to the servants. 'Do what He tells you,' she says, taking control for her friends' sake. And He saves the situation. How delightfully true to life, and how free from intrusion of theology.

So is the rest. Awkward groomsmen have made bad jokes from then till now, and everybody has laughed. The master of the feast made a bad joke: 'Not like the rest of them,' he said, 'who keep their old vinegar till the company is past noticing.' Not a good quip, but how naive and natural, how true to the rustic simplicity of the nuptial occasion. There is nothing here to mar the graciousness of guest or son.

MARY AND MARTHA

Pursue the charge of ungraciousness a little further. There is a story in chapter ten of Luke's gospel:

> A woman named Martha (runs the story, idiomatically translated) received Him into her house. And her sister Mary sat at Jesus' feet and was listening to what He had to say. Martha, distracted with much serving, came and stood over them and said, 'Master, do You not care that my sister has left me alone to do the work? Tell her now to take a hand with me.' Jesus replied, 'Martha, Martha, you are troubled and upset over many things. One thing you need; and that good part Mary has chosen, and it shall not be taken away from her.'

So runs the story. The good part was a reference to such banqueting customs as we find in Genesis 43:34. Martha is not blamed, but gently shown that service which distracts and frays the temper is not to be preferred to quiet attentiveness; unruffled attention to what the Master has to say leads to truest service. The rush of even laudable business can destroy the spirit's calm so that the service itself loses its effectiveness. Mary had realized that 'man lives not by bread alone;' and there is no truth more essential, none that she needed more. Without this 'good part,' the feast of life loses its spiritual vitamin. Service begins at the feet of Jesus; so the story becomes a parable of Christian usefulness.

Oddly enough, John himself obliquely comments on this story. He wrote a generation later than Matthew. In his account is recorded the raising of Lazarus. Over the years the old apostle may have met with glib misunderstanding about the incident in the Bethany home. His theme took him to that same place, for he was to tell the story of Lazarus. There is a touch of delicate appreciation of her in the Lazarus story, for, introducing his theme, John wrote, 'Now Jesus loved Martha, and her sister, and Lazarus'. If one could only know whether Martha was still alive when John wrote his letter, whether she was, in fact, 'the lady' mentioned in the second epistle of John, a most intriguingly human touch would be added to the story. John writes as if he was a little weary of those who saw no virtue in the practical Martha and perhaps excused their lack in hospitality and courtesy toward guests on the grounds of Christ's words.

INCIDENT IN TYRE

In Matthew 15:21–29, Jesus makes an unexplained visit to Tyre. It seemed unmotivated, save that He sought needed rest. It was His one excursion out of the true territory of Israel. A track led over the hills out of Galilee to a point near Tyre, a track now closed by the hostile Lebanese border. In Tyre there is a well-laid first century pavement on which the Lord may have trodden between the columned arcades of a shopping street. Why did He make this northern journey? All day the men who walked with Him may have murmured about the Gentiles—these 'dogs' unworthy of 'the children's bread'. They disliked this foray into Phoenicia.

Then in the Tyrian street the Gentile woman importuned Him. Try to imagine the scene. Dark-faced, the disciples looked on. The quick-witted Phoenician saw their opposition and caught the warmth of His kindliness. Perhaps He had brought them north for precisely this lesson. Turning to them, He spoke the words in Matthew 15:26 with a note of sorrow and irony in His voice, 'I mustn't take the children's bread and give it to *dogs*'. The woman caught His words up cleverly and said, with a side look at the disapproving men, 'To be sure, but the little dogs eat of the bits which fall from the *children's table'*. Imagine a slight ironical emphasis on *children's*.

Build such a plausible, or rather a meaningful context, and the incident falls into place. Otto Borchert, in his splendid book on the person of Christ, *The Original Jesus*, argues that irony does not go with greatness. He is wrong here. Socrates used a kindly irony. Christ used irony as a tool of kindliness and as a gentle weapon of rebuke. Observe Luke 5:32. Christ was speaking to the Pharisees who had been carping at His association with 'publicans and sinners'. In irony and sorrow, He said, 'I came not to call the righteous, but sinners to repentance. They who are whole need no physician'. The tone of the words is all important, and written language lacks devices to represent the whole range of emphases in the spoken voice. Touch *righteous* and *whole* with slightest ironical emphasis; perhaps put the lightest of stress on the word *sinners*. The righteous were the Pharisees, the self-styled saints, and how righteous were they?

TEMPLE COURT

What now of anger? It is difficult to be angry without sin. Paul says in Ephesians 4:26, 'Be ye angry, and sin not'. Is the phrase a justification of sharp temper? Is it a contradiction in language? He meant, of course, 'Be angry *but* sin not'. Both Latin and Greek often fail to distinguish between the copulative and the adversative conjunctions *and* and *but*. Paul recognizes, in other words, the existence of righteous anger. Anger can only be righteous when it is anger against wickedness and completely unselfish, when it is a spark from the wrath of God. The Lord cleansing the temple was righteously angry. In Matthew 23, in the eloquent denunciation of Pharisaic sham and double-dealing, we have another illustration. The Lord was angry, but sinned not. The question is, of course, whether any anger in our own imperfect humanity can be quite unselfish. Subtle reactions of self-esteem, and self-righteousness enter into our apparently most unselfish and most justified bursts of indignation. How can we be sure that our anger is sinless? We simply cannot. That is why Paul adds, 'Let not the sun go down upon your wrath'. Read the verses in Way's translation. Here they are, 'In your anger let there be no sin. Let not the sun go down while yet your wrath is hot. Nay, give the devil no such vantage ground.'

We shall look now more closely at the story in John 2. Any attentive reader of the four gospels cannot fail to note that Christ's cleansing of the temple is significantly reported by each one of them. The four writers saw the naked truth that from the moment of His valiant protest against commercialized religion, the Master was doomed. To clash with the priestly promoters of the 'house of merchandise' was death. The market in the sacred place was a Sadducean enterprise.

The story is worth retelling if only for its disturbing relevance. Not once but many times has errant man followed the path that leads so easily to self-seeking and found, under the altar's very shadow, the temptation to make a profit.

Arriving in Jerusalem for the Passover, Jesus made His way through the narrow streets to the open forecourt of Herod's great temple, the court of the Gentiles as the Jews called it. A noisy and unseemly spectacle greeted Him.

Victims for the Jewish ritual of sacrifice were required, lambs for the Passover meal, as well as for the symbolic offering of purification, bullocks for a major sacrifice, and turtledoves to supply the poor man's less expensive offering. The proud priestly caste, left in office by the Romans at the price of subservience and collaboration, had seen the gleam of shekels in the situation. Ostensibly for the convenience of worshippers but in reality as a great commercial venture, they had instituted a cattle market in the sacred precincts. It was an astute but disgraceful trick to secure a cynical double gain; the flesh of the sacrificed beasts was a priestly prerequisite; and what they had sold for profit in the court they received back again for nothing at the altar.

Reeking similarly of the ways of racketeers, was the money exchange they had set up in the same enclosure. Jews came for the Passover from all the world, like Moslems to modern Mecca. Simon, who carried the cross, was a Jew from Cyrene in distant Libya, and the list of those who heard Peter's sermon covers loyal visitors from all over the Mediterranean world. These visitors carried in their pouches the heathen money of Rome or Greece. Gifts to the temple and the tax required of every adult Israelite, rich or poor, were payable only in Jewish coinage. The sacerdotal corporations established the rate of exchange. Perhaps the squared marks in the flagstones at Capernaum are such a 'table' as they used.

Such was the scene of hypocrisy and commerce in the holy place. Christ made, we are told, a whip of small cords, drove the animals out, and overturned the tables of the money changers. A little imagination can reconstruct the scene.

The famous picture of the flailing whip in active, passionate hands is incorrect. The mind rejects it as incongruous. Rather, from the cluttered pavement He gathered a handful of the trampled strands of rope cast

aside by those who had penned and corralled the cattle.
Holding His rough scourge conspicuously in hand, He
walked quietly into the midst of the courtyard and looked
sternly around Him. Strange tales were abroad about the
Galilean. There was odd power in His presence, and in
more than one uneasy mind of those who watched,
oracles of the Old Testament remembered from school
and synagogue, rose accusingly. 'The Lord whom ye seek
shall suddenly come to His temple; even the messenger of
the covenant . . . saith the Lord of Hosts.' It is well
known that the temper of those who control them is
communicated for good or ill to beasts. Any horse can
disconcertingly gauge his rider's fear or confidence. The
whip, too, was the symbol of man's domination of the
animal, and no reader of the ancient stories can fail to see
the awesome power the personality of Christ held for
those who loved and those who hated Him alike.

He stood quietly and looked at them. Uneasiness
spread through stall and pen. Suddenly, sensing the
disturbance and the uncanniness of the lull as conversation died on a hundred lips and men halted anxiously in
their activities, a sheep or bullock broke for the gate. Any
drover knows how the panic of one can precipitate a
stampede. The flocks and herds rushed for the open.
Right and left, the tables of the money changers were
flung jingling to the flagstones. 'Take these things hence,'
He said to the sellers of doves. And to the cowed and
glaring attendants of the priestly cattle market, He
added with scorn, 'Make not my Father's house a house
of merchandise'.

There was no violence, no lashing in anger, only the
tremendous power of His presence. Significantly in proof
of this interpretation, those who sought cause to remove
Him found no charge of violence to level against Him.

The world too readily forgets the sterner side of Jesus Christ. They remember Him as the babe of Mary, the lover of children, the compassionate protector of broken womankind, the brave friend of the outcast and the pariah, and the forgiving Saviour of the cross. All this is true and Christian. But Christ was also the ruthless flayer of hypocrisy; the merciless critic of sham, pretence, and insincerity; and the uncompromising foe of exploitation and the ever waiting greed for gain, which at Christmas time still turns the Gentile courtyard of that holy day into a place of sordid merchandise. On all these things, Christ would look, as He did at the cattle, the crowding sheep, the piles of drachmas, denarii, and silver shekels with burning eye—and the whip of small cords.

THE PHARISEES

If Christ was without sin, it follows that He could be angry without the self-righteous exaltation which mars the virtue of any human show of indignation. So it was that He could denounce the Pharisees as He does in the long philippic of Matthew 23. Milton, the grand old reformer of Puritanism, will be sufficient comment. In his *Apology for Smectymnuus* he writes,

> For in times of opposition, when against new heresies arising, or old corruptions to be reformed, this cool impassionate mildness of positive wisdom, is not enough to dam and astonish the proud resistance of carnal and false doctors, then (that I may have leave to soar a while, as the poets do) Zeal, whose substance is ethereal, arming in complete diamond, ascends his fiery chariot, drawn by two blazing meteors, figured like beasts, but of a higher breed than any zodiac yields, resembling those four which Ezekiel and St. John saw—the one visaged like a lion to express power, high

authority, and indignation, the other of man, to cast derision and scorn upon perverse and fraudulent seducers—with them the invincible warrior, Zeal, shaking loosely the slack reins, drives over the heads of scarlet prelates and such as are insolent to maintain traditions, bruising their stiff necks under his flaming wheels. Thus did the true prophets of old combat with the false; thus Christ, Himself the fountain of meekness, found acrimony enough to be still galling and vexing the prelatical Pharisees. But ye will say, these had immediate warrant from God to be thus bitter; and I say, so much the plainer is it found that there may be a sanctified bitterness against the enemies of the truth.[3]

Old-fashioned words, but Milton touches the truth.

Fig Tree

But turn back to chapter 21 in the same gospel, Matthew. Did the Lord curse the barren fig tree in petulance or anger? No. It was parable in action. Eastern teachers taught by actions as well as words. There are many illustrations in the prophets who married wives, hid girdles, made yokes, and gave many other object lessons. The Lord, too, 'set a child in the midst,' and in parable as well as indignation drove out the money changers. Only a few weeks before (Lk 13:6), He had used the barren fig tree to illustrate Israel's fruitlessness. Now He significantly repeated the lesson and made it wider in its meaning, for it also illustrates the spiritual truths of the sermon on the vine (Jn 15:6). Here was the tree, like many a man, green with the leaves of profession, but with no fruit of rich reality beneath. It was a living hypocrisy. By its withering, the Lord showed that visible death and ugliness, apparent for all to see, is the final end of backsliding. If we cease to produce the fruits of the Spirit (Gal 5:22), though the outward habits and formalities of our religion may maintain appearances for some brief time, the sham must ultimately be exposed. In the national application, the destruction of Jerusalem, with the Roman Titus as 'the axe' (Is 10:15), was the outworking of the prophetic lesson.

HATING PARENTS

But what of His attitude to family relationships? Does the Lord's word in Luke 14:26 forbid filial affection in the follower of Christ? No. It is perfectly certain that He who bade His followers love their enemies would not have prescribed hatred of parents. He was speaking in terms of comparative loyalty. He was speaking, too, in the colourful language of Eastern thought. Hyperbole is natural in Hebrew and Arabic. So also is vivid and concrete illustration. No Eastern hearer of the precept concerning the 'second mile' and the 'cloke also,' would misunderstand so far as to obey this hyperbolic injunction literally. He would readily understand that the figure of speech commanded only extreme longsuffering and sacrificial generosity. And all would see, with a readiness we exact and logical Northerners or Westerners will not find easy to understand, that the precept which speaks of hatred of one's parents means only that, when affections clash, loyalty to God must come first. 'Let me first bury my father,' one said, meaning, 'Let me wait until my father dies.' 'An earthly affection,' said the Lord, 'must not bind us thus.' (Compare Mt 10:35–42.) And what of His own brothers? In John 7:8 where the Lord says, 'I go not up to this feast,' does He deceive them? In the next verse He appears to go. There is no deception. Christ described Himself as truth incarnate. No lie or subterfuge ever marred the honesty of His character. We can start from this point. If He appears in this one passage to contradict His nature, the passage must be wrongly reported or wrongly read. We must lack background or circumstantial context. There are two possible explanations. First emphasize *this*, and then suppose that the ensuing narrative is highly condensed. Perhaps, as David Smith maintains, the Lord did not go up to 'this' feast, but set out behind His brethren on the leisurely journey which was to bring Him to the Passover feast. Or perhaps the minority of manuscripts which read 'not yet' retain the correct reading. If we could read, 'I go not yet up to this feast,' the whole difficulty is immediately removed. It is probable that the former explanation is to be preferred.

While on the same theme, glance at Luke 8:19–21 where Christ seems to reject His brothers along with His mother when they sought to reach Him through the surging crowd. Before imagining harshness in His attitude, consider both the brevity and the purpose of the story. There are fifty-six words in the Greek text. The visitors were not necessarily rejected nor dismissed unkindly without seeing Him; we do not know what happened. The Lord obviously did delay the commencement of His ministry until Mary's other children were sufficiently mature to sustain her or be no burden upon her resources. He saw to it that Mary was cared for even in the midst of the agony of His end. This story is related, after the fashion in which John, the other evangelist, chooses his incidental narrative—to highlight an important saying. He uses the occasion to speak of the brotherhood and relationship of all believers, and it is a fact of experience that those who are one in Christ can be more intimately linked than blood relations who do not share their faith.

BRUSQUENESS

The terse rebuke in Luke 12:13–14 to a man who brought an obsessive problem of injustice to Christ must be looked at in its context. The crowds were surging round, and it seems, from the drift of a highly condensed narrative, that a man interrupted a serious discourse on dependence on God with an untimely intrusion. Deaf to immortal words which he might have heard to his eternal profit, the fellow blundered tactlessly and publicly forward with his private financial problem. All he could think about, in the presence of Christ, was money. Hence a deserved rebuke.

GOOD MASTER

Another matter to clear in the context of this discussion is the incident described in Mark 10:17–31. The young man in the story caught a glimpse of truth. The discovery stirred him to the depths. Here on the road with His band of disciples was the One who could help him. He cast reserve and respectability aside, ran, and knelt. 'Good Master,' he cried, 'what must I do to win a part in eternal life?'

In this illuminating story, several points must be noted. The first is the unwillingness of Christ to take advantage of a state of emotional excitement. Christ's followers, likewise, should take care not to use mere emotion to secure decision.

Abiding conviction must be based on reason. It must count first the cost of decision. It must follow calm and deliberate choice. Christ saw that the youth kneeling in the road was overwrought. He was not himself. He proceeded to strip the self-deception away. '*Why* do you call me good?' he asked. The emphasis is on the interro-

gative. The question was no disclaimer of goodness. He
paused and prompted the silent young man. '*Why* do you
call me good? . . . There is no one good but God.'

The right answer lay ready. He might have replied,
'Master, I have heard that one of Your men said You
were the Christ, the Son of the living God, that You
accepted His Word. I call You good because I know that
You are the Messiah; I call You good because God is
good, and You have said that You and He are one. This
is not a courtesy tag I might use to any rabbi of the
synagogue. I call You good because You are my Saviour.
To my Saviour, the Messiah of Israel, I address my
question: what must I do to inherit eternal life?'

On this foundation the Lord might have built. Christianity must begin with the recognition of the lordship
and deity of Christ. There is no Christianity with a
Christ who is less than God. A saint, a martyr, might
inspire and daunt us, but could not save. The young man
might have had his answer there and then, but failed to
grasp the truth.

The rest of the conversation demonstrates the Lord's
endeavour to prompt the mood which might have led to
blessing and the boon the young man groped for. He had
failed to reply adequately. The Lord, still determined not
to bypass the will and clear conviction of the inquirer,
turned to the old familiar pathway of the law. He quoted
the fifth to the ninth commandments, adding 'defraud
not,' a precept from Deuteronomy (24:14) referring to
prompt payment of an employee's wages, doubtless
relevant in the case of a man with a large establishment.

Again the young man might have replied correctly.
Had he conceived the law aright, in the terms perhaps of
the Sermon on the Mount, or in the manner which
provided, a generation later, some of the most passionate

confessions of Paul, he would have replied, 'Master, I know the law and have tried as long as I can remember to meet its demands. All I find is despair and frustration. The law does not save me from sin, it merely underlines my sin. There is a law in my members warring against the law of my mind. I need not a code but a saviour. Be merciful, Lord, to me a sinner.'

He said none of this. The puzzled face looked up, 'Master, I have done all these things.' The law had not done its work of conviction in him. He had confused respectability with goodness. Morality for him was passive, a mere abstaining. It was not active, a drive to do. What a pity. We all know such people and covet them for Christ, but their sheer blamelessness, in the accepted sense, is a barrier between them and Him. The Lord 'looked at him and loved him'. There is yearning in the phrase and His longing to break through and make the self-satisfied youth see and understand the shallowness of the outer rectitude he prized.

MAN OF SORROWS

It is alleged that Christ never laughed. This is an ancient observation found even in the medieval letter of Publius Lentulus, an alleged description of Jesus.* Wit is evident in the sayings of the Lord, but though He wept, no word records His laughter. Happiness is not hilarity, nor is joy necessarily on the superficial level of happiness. Socrates ended life with a jest; but we would not expect that on Calvary. The burden of the world's pain lay too heavily upon Him for the light mood which breeds fun and humour to be His common mood.

*See Appendix 1 for this document.

Juvenal writes of Democritus, the 'laughing philosopher' of Abdera (460–370 B.C.) and Heracleitus, of a century earlier, the 'dark philosopher' of Ephesus:

> Come do we now approve the story told
> Of those philosophers who lived of old?
> The one would laugh and laugh whene'er he stepped
> Outside his house, the other always wept.
> Yes all can laugh. To me not yet appears
> What fount supplied all Heracleitus' tears.
> Democritus, at every step abroad
> With merriment and ribald laughter roared.[4]

Horace Walpole remarked that life is a comedy to those who think, a tragedy to those who feel. Jesus came closer to the second group, closer to the stricken Heracleitus. It takes nothing from either His manliness or His perfection that He did not laugh. It graces Him—He cared.

TEMPTATION

Temptation is not sin. Jesus Christ was tempted 'yet without sin' (Heb 4:15). But temptation was real and rending. Behind the palms, cypress and jacaranda of the town of Jericho, a mile back from the arid mound which covers the remains of a dozen ancient fortresses, stands a bare mountain on the edge of the Judean wilderness. This is the traditional place of Christ's temptation.

How was He to conduct His ministry? As the wonder-worker, able to feed a hungry multitude and turn the stones to bread? The multitudes will follow those who feed them, as He Himself once said (Jn 6:26). Was He to seek the path of worldly influence and power in wider spheres than the little land? And as He wrestled with this thought, perhaps He saw what He had often seen from the high uplifted edge of hills where Nazareth stood. The vast, level floor of Esdraelon lies beneath. It was a highway of all nations; Egyptian, Assyrian, Babylonian, Greek and Roman had marched that way. Alive and vivid in His memory was the vision of the kingdoms of the world seen again 'in a moment of time'. Palestine was small, obscure, trampled by vast empires.

Should He stand aloft on the temple top and shatter all the scorn and incredulity of men by demonstrating His faith in Scripture and His own Messiahship? The storm raged through Him, for He was tempted in all ways as we are (Heb 4:15). It is only those who do not yield who know the ultimate impact of testing.

Matthew changes the order of the trials. Temptation is repetitive, varied, resourceful. A mind is behind temptation, organizing the attack, in open confrontation or in ambush, varying the assault, probing for the weak places, returning, switching the attacking thrust now here, now there. For long weeks it continued, as He threw back the fierce invasion and answered with Scripture each twisted argument.

Had this experience of evil's drag, thrust and power not been included in the story, He would have been much less real in His humanity. Indeed, as the writer to the Hebrews was led perceptively to say, how much would have been subtracted from His Saviourhood (Heb 4:15).

The Nazarenes

Why then, some have argued, did it come about that Jesus' fellow townsmen fulfilled Isaiah's prophecy and 'found no beauty in him that they should desire him' (Is 53:2), or as Moffatt turned the phrase, 'He had no beauty to attract our eyes, no charm to make us choose him'? He failed to impress Nazareth, even met danger there, and 'could do no great work among them because of their unbelief'. It is the common fashion of men to measure others by themselves, and to dislike preeminence in those they know. Jealousy haunts the human heart and denies tribute to those who lives have run a mutual path. But there are deeper reasons, and no one has put it better than the saintly Blaise Pascal, two centuries ago, in his perceptive *Pensées*.

> It is not in this manner that he chose to appear in the gentleness of his coming; because since so many men had become unworthy of his clemency, he wished them to suffer the privation of the good that they did not want. It would not have been right therefore for him to appear in a way that was plainly divine and absolutely bound to convince all mankind; but it was not right either that he should come in a manner so hidden that he could not be recognized by those who sought him sincerely. He chose to make himself perfectly knowable to them; and thus, wishing to appear openly to those who seek him with all their heart, and hidden from those who flee him with all their heart, he tempered the knowledge of himself, with the result that he has given signs of himself which are visible to those who seek him, and not to those who do not seek him.[5]

The same situation is distinguishable, as Dr. A. J. Hoover of Los Angeles points out, in other times than those in which men and women made immediate contact with Christ. 'History may be an ideal way for God to "temper" the knowledge of Himself so that He is partly revealed and partly concealed. The person seeking God may rejoice at what is revealed, however partial, but the person fleeing God will use the partial to justify his unbelief.'[6] In any other age but their own the Nazarenes would be counted among the latter class. As Pascal goes on to say, 'There is light enough for those who desire only to see, and darkness enough for those of a contrary disposition.'

CONCLUSION

There is no more to be said. Jesus emerges from a careful scrutiny of the gospels a unique being, uncontaminated by the world around Him, yet in no sense shunning it or protecting Himself from contact and near association with it. He was involved in life, yet not marred by it; in it, yet apart; a man, but more than a man.

Allow two friends, two who ran together to an empty tomb in the murk of the morning, to provide a last testimony.

'When Jesus came to the district of Caesarea Philippi, He asked His disciples, "Who do men say that the Son of man is?" They replied, "Some say John the Baptist, others Elijah, and yet others Jeremiah or one of the prophets." He said to them, "And you, what do you say?" Peter replied, "You are the Messiah, the Son of the Living God"' (Mt 16:13–17; Mk 8:27–29; Lk 9:18–21; Jn 6:68–69, author's paraphrase).

Peter was dead thirty years when John summed up the whole of the New Testament in the prologue to his gospel. He wrote with the knowledge of a century in his mind. He had seen the first victories of the Christian faith. He had suffered in his person for what he taught and like Paul had reached the serenity which knew whom he had believed.

Here, then, are John's words in answer to the question of this book. I have translated them afresh, with acknowledgment to J. B. Phillips for a phrase in verse 16:

> In the beginning was Mind, a mind which expressed itself. That mind was with God, indeed was God, and existed with God from all time.

All matter came into being through Him. Apart from Him no single thing was created. In Him was life, and this life was the light of mankind. The light still shines in the darkness, and the darkness has never quenched it.

There was a man called John, who came to tell the truth about the light, so that everyone should come to faith through him. He was not the light himself. He was simply a witness to it, to the true light which shines upon every man coming into the world.

He came into the world, the world which owed its being to Him, and the world did not recognize Him. He came home, and His own people would not take Him in. But to any who did receive Him, to them He gave the right and privilege to become the children of God, to those who had faith in His name, born not as we are born into life on earth, but born again of God by faith.

So God expressed Himself in human flesh and lived for a time among us. We saw His splendour, that of the Father's only Son, full of grace and truth. It was about Him that John testified, 'This is the One,' he said, 'of whom I was speaking, the One who was before me but came after me, for He lived before I was born.'

Of His abundance we all shared, with grace in our lives because of the grace in His. Moses indeed gave the law, but grace and truth came with Jesus Christ. No one has ever seen God. The divine Son, who can never be separated from the Father, has shown what God is like (Jn 1:1–18).

8

Implications and a Personal Challenge

The implications of this examination and the personal challenge which arises if the gospels are thus read.

BY WAY OF EPILOGUE

John's prologue may have been the last words of the Bible to be written. He had filled a whole papyrus roll, the common unit of measure in all ancient publications. It had been a weary task for an old man. On Patmos, whose high hump lay mauve upon the horizon, he had seen his Master clad in glory and told of Him and the future in poetry mingled with the scenes of his island exile: the sea, bright as though mixed with fire, which ran like a glassy plain out into the setting sun, the high cumulus shot with lightning like a throne of God, the ever present murmur of many waters.

He was tired, and the century, just relieved of the grim person of Domitian, was weary too. John had written his last message. Remembered words of Paul, dead almost thirty years, were tangled with what he had written. Much more than he had written thronged his memory. 'Of course,' he wrote, 'Jesus did many other notable and significant deeds, and His disciples witnessed them personally, but what has been written here has one purpose, that you may believe that Jesus was the Messiah, and that, holding such faith, you should have the life He came to give' (Jn 20:21; Jn 21:25).

Then the old man found his book was not finished after all. It is not possible to guess how long a gap lay between his writing of those words and the addition to his manuscript of that fine story of a dawn by Galilee and the curiously enigmatic conversation between the Lord and Peter and John. It was necessary, however, to set the record right. Odd rumours were abroad. So John added his postscript and ended whimsically, 'There are many other things which Jesus did, and if they were all written in detail, I think the whole world would not hold the books' (Jn 21:25).

One might guess that it was after the writing of the last chapter (or the next-to-last one) that John wrote the eighteen verses which introduce his book. But whenever he wrote them, he put the whole meaning of the Bible into those few score words. Historians have pursued a quest for many personalities of history through documents, traditions and reports. They have sought Socrates behind what three men wrote of him. They have pierced the mist of prejudiced hostility which Tacitus spread over the person of Tiberius and learned to understand that able and embittered man. In such discovery and understanding such quests of scholarship end.

We have sought the reality of Jesus Christ. We can never know Him as the last living man to remember and write about Him knew Him, but our conclusion must contain the implications John set down. It is not enough to satisfy ourselves that Jesus was an historical figure, even that He was a unique person without parallel, an extraordinary being of dimensions unknown before in history. The investigator is presented with a challenge and a choice. Something is demanded of one who finds that Jesus is no product of His times, an intrusion into history rather than an actor in it. Clearly His words must be heard, for His story becomes significant and convincing in the context of His claims and the revelation of His person.

A PERSONAL MATTER

We who read and examine are thrust into a place of decision. The matter cannot pause at some historical or some merely intellectual conclusion. It calls for action. Who was Jesus? God's revelation of Himself, His last utterance of truth, His final Word to man. It is acceptance of that fact, faith that in Christ God is discoverable, and (the logical consequence) a personal committal to all this belief implies that constitutes the whole challenge of the Christian faith. Like the procurator of Judea, we face a crisis, and remembering that the very word *krisis* in Greek means a judgment, we are confronted by the realization that the story judges us rather than we the story.

We face God in action—no theological concept, abstract 'ground of being,' or undemanding 'ultimate reality,' but a God involved, if Calvary means anything, a God pursuing. It is as Lewis once remarked:

> An impersonal God—well and good. A subjective God of beauty, truth and goodness, inside our own heads, better still. A formless life-force surging through us, a vast power which we can tap—best of all. But God Himself, alive, pulling at the other end of the cord, perhaps approaching at infinite speed . . . that is quite another matter . . . So it is a sort of Rubicon. One goes across; or not.[1]

And as with Julius Caesar when he cried, 'The die is cast,' and splashed his horse across the silt-laden little stream which was the border of his province, from that moment it is war.

But look again at the last words of John's twentieth chapter, with which he first thought to close his book. 'To have life in His name,' to have the life His very Person guarantees, is the gift which the Bible calls salvation. Jesus lived, and Jesus Christ is Saviour. There is an enslavement which destroys all freedom unless emancipation can be found. Fail in life to discover that freedom, and the mind and heart are prone to man's endemic malady, frustration and despair; for it is true, as the Pursuer cries in Francis Thompson's poem that 'all things betray thee who betrayest Me.'[2] For multitudes, hell is no theme of theological disputation. It is here, woven with the very circumstances of life, closing in, and vainly fled in drugs, drink, manifold perversion, and excess, escape to the desert, to fantasy, and to self-destruction.

Salvation means quiet of mind and heart, purpose that uses each day's reborn energy, the recovery of significance, a happiness which finds meaning in all experience; the 'life more abundantly' of Christ's own promise. 'Something lives,' as the hymn says, 'in every hue, Christless eyes have never seen.' As Francis Thompson also said, in another poem:

'Tis ye, 'tis your estranged faces
That miss the many-splendoured thing.[3]

And salvation contains the serene confidence that all such meaning, purpose and joy cannot be bounded and confined by the narrow limits of this brief life. The 'eternal life' of John's common phrase is a life which here and now knows God, and must therefore be beyond destruction.

I, who have sought to lead you through these pages, search for a conclusion and appeal, and feel, as I have found before, that words fall short in such communication. In such a theme, how can the austere aloofness of objective scholarship be guarded and preserved? How can one who has found in personal faith, outworked in life's thousand contexts, that Christ is Saviour, do less than urge upon those to whom he speaks, or for whom he writes, the trial of an experiment? The resurrection is historic fact, and on its basis rests the present reality of a living Christ. He can still be blessedly encountered, and a Christian can do no less than testify to that reality, and press the subjects of his interest and concern, his fellow-men and women, to accept that confrontation in some place of prayer, some moment of outreaching, some step of acceptance, committal and faith.

A poem which I once heard stays in my mind. Its author I have never discovered. Nor had the headmaster I once met in Cape Town, to whom it had once come with similar challenge. It is simple enough verse, of no great literary merit, that I almost hesitate to quote, lest some should think that the words take too lightly the difficulties which for some strew the path of faith. But here it is, slightly abbreviated:

> *I had walked life's way with an easy tread,*
> *Had followed where comforts and pleasure led,*
> *With station and rank and wealth for my goal,*
> *Much thought for my body but none for my soul,*
> *I had entered to win in life's mad race,*
> *When I met the Master face to face . . .*
> *And I faltered and fell at His feet that day*
> *While my castles melted and vanished away,*
> *And I cried aloud, 'O make me meet*
> *To follow the steps of Thy wounded feet.'*
> *My thought is now for the souls of men;*
> *I have lost my life to find it again,*
> *E'er since one day in a quiet place*
> *I met the Master face to face.*

Sentiments too lush for our Anglo-Saxon reserve in matters of religion, an overplay of the emotions? Some may think so, but there are others who will richly understand. Life's deeper experiences involve the emotions; witness Paul on the Damascus road, Augustine in the garden at Milan.

Or look at Spurgeon in the little chapel at Colchester. The preaching that snowy morning in 1850 was crude. The lay preacher in the high pulpit could do little more than reiterate his text: 'Look unto me and be ye saved, all the ends of the earth.' There were few present in the wild winter weather, and that perhaps is why the stumbling preacher addressed the listening boy under the little gallery personally: 'Young man, look to Jesus Christ and live.' Spurgeon wrote later, 'I looked until I could almost have looked my eyes away. There and then the cloud was gone, and at that moment I saw the sun.'

Who was Jesus? When history has answered, the last word lies with each of us.

What Jesus Looked Like

The appearance of Jesus has always been a matter of speculation, and a long, but not necessarily reliable, tradition may be traced from the art of the catacombs to the spurious letter of Publius Lentulus. This document, written in very passable Latin, first appeared around the fourteenth century. It purported to be a report from Publius Lentulus, a Roman officer in Judea at the time of Christ. It is quite without authority, and the picture it presents is derived from representations in later Roman-Christian art when the severer philosophic type became prevalent.

> His countenance is severe and expressive, so as to inspire beholders at once with love and with fear . . . In reproving, he is awe-inspiring, in exhorting and teaching, his speech is gentle and caressing. His expression is of wonderful sweetness and gravity. No one ever saw him laugh, but he has often been seen to weep. [The description includes hair] falling in graceful curls to the shoulders . . . a forehead smooth and large, cheeks of lovely red, a nose and mouth of exquisite symmetry, a beard, thick and of a pale colour . . . parted in the middle like a fork.

One observes the intrusion of Aryan features.

In the rough art of the catacombs, Jesus is shown as the good Shepherd, opening the eyes of the blind, healing the woman with the issue of blood, and blessing a child. He is invariably shown youthful and beardless, and, as far as one can be dogmatic about art so simple, of gentle and benign expression. Nothing is shown, save what can be guessed from Scripture and, on that basis, some of the Fathers have built a tradition of ignoble appearance, uncomeliness, and ugliness. Justin Martyr, Tertullian, Clement, Origen and Basil agree in this dishonourable tradition with no shadow of authority except Isaiah 52. Jerome, on the other hand, with another patristic group following rather the Song of Songs and some prophetic psalms, argued for a quite contrary tradition of comeliness. Chrysostom, Gregory of Nyssa, Ambrose and Augustine were at one in this.

No authentic portrait of Christ was recognized by the early church, though Eusebius said that he had seen portraits of Jesus, Peter and Paul. The same Eusebius, however, gives credence to a tradition about a statue at Caesarea Philippi that supposedly bore the likeness of Jesus. It is more likely to have been Vespasian or Hadrian, if the statue actually existed, with the suppliant province in the form of a woman bowed before him. Imagination read into it the story of Luke. The portraits he reported are probably no more reliable.

The oldest surviving likeness is one in imitation mosaic removed to the Vatican museum from the catacomb of Saint Callixtus. It is probably from the fourth century—as far removed from genuine memory as we are from Shakespeare. The mosaic portrays a smooth-browed adult with long, brown hair, large, thoughtful eyes, long, narrow nose, and serene countenance. The spurious Lentulus epistle may have derived something from it.

The early Christians probably had a deep inhibition against all such portraiture, and the fact that the emperor Alexander Severus had images of Christ along with those of Abraham and Orpheus in his household *lararium* is indication enough that the fear was justified.

Representation in portrait and mosaic became common enough with the coming of the church buildings and basilicas, but have no historical value. There is even a mosaic picture of Christ dating back to the fourth or fifth century that was dug up on a villa site at Hinton St. Mary in Dorset. At least, it shows a male portrait associated in the design with the chi-rho sign. The portrait adds nothing to our knowledge.

We must conclude that we know nothing from art, archaeology or description of the appearance of Christ. Ancient historians were not given to detailed physical descriptions. The evangelists saw no need to describe One whose appearance was familiar. However, such portraiture, up to and beyond the fourth century—a period not marred and interrupted by cultural and widespread civil breakdown—is a cogent argument in itself for historicity.[1]

Relevant Historical Data

SOME RELEVANT DATES

(Many dates are necessarily conjectural.)

B.C.

5 Presumed date of the postponed 'enrolment' in Palestine, and consequently of the nativity. Birth of Seneca at Corduba in Spain.

4 Death of Herod. Archelaus, Herod Antipas and Philip divide his realm.

3 The holy family returns from Egypt.

A.D.

6 Banishment of Archelaus. Coponius becomes procurator of the new province of Judea.

7 The census of Acts 5:34.

14 Death of Augustus (in August). Tiberius becomes emperor.

26 Tiberius retires to Capri. Seianus is in virtual control in Rome. Pontius Pilatus becomes procurator of Palestine, succeeding Valerius Gratus.

29 Presumed date of the crucifixion.

30 Velleius Paterculus publishes his history.

32 Martyrdom of Stephen(?). Expansion of the church into Samaria.

33 Conversion of Paul.

34 Death of Philip, tetrarch of Ituraea.

35 Pilate's massacre in Samaria.

36 Intervention of Vitellius, legate of Syria, and dismissal of Pilate. Marullus becomes procurator.

37 Death of Tiberius. Accession of Gaius Caligula. Birth of Nero and Josephus. Herod Agrippa I succeeds to Philip's tetrarchy.

38   The church, now established in Antioch, begins its Gentile ministry. Riots in Alexandria between Jews and Gentiles.
39   Herod Antipas is deposed and exiled. Birth of Lucan.
41   Assassination of Gaius. Accession of Claudius. Herod Agrippa I, with royal title, succeeds to all the old Herodian realms.
42   Herod Agrippa's persecution of the church (?).
43   Roman invasion of Britain.
44   Martyrdom of James. Death of Herod Agrippa I. Reversion to procuratorial rule in Palestine. Cuspius Fadus is appointed. Seneca actively writing, as was Phaedrus the minor poet and fabulist (possibly earlier).
46   Paul and Barnabas are in Jerusalem. Tiberius Alexander, nephew of Philo, is procurator of Judaea.
47   First mission to Galatia. Vespasian and Titus consolidate in Britain.
48   Execution of Messalina, Claudius' wife. Claudius marries Agrippina. Ventidius Cumanus becomes procurator of Judaea. Herod Agrippa becomes king of Chalcis.
49   Jerusalem Council (?). Claudius expels the Jews from Rome. First Christian evangelism in Rome. Seneca returns from exile to be Nero's tutor. Paul reaches Europe.
50   Paul is in Corinth. Claudius adopts Nero, Agrippina's son.
51   Gallio arrives in Corinth.
52   Cumanus is recalled and succeeded as procurator by Antonius Felix. The first letter to Corinth is written this year or the next.
53   Herod Agrippa becomes Agrippa II, ruling the consolidated domains of Philip and Lysanias. Marriage of Nero and Octavia, daughter of Claudius. Paul is in Ephesus.
54   Death of Claudius. Accession of Nero. Felix marries Drusilla.
55   Epistle to the Romans is written about this date.
56   Paul's visit to Jerusalem and his arrest.
57   Accusation of Pomponia Graecina in Rome on charge of 'foreign superstition'. Christianity penetrates aristocracy (?).
58   Felix is recalled. Porcius Festus becomes procurator. Paul appeals to Caesar.
59   Nero murders Agrippina, his mother. Paul reaches Rome.
60   Epistles to Philemon, Colossians, Ephesians, Philippians are written in Rome. Also, Luke's gospel and the Acts are taking shape. Mark's gospel is begun. Columella publishes his book on farming.

61 Younger Pliny is born.
62 Acquittal of Paul (?). Death of Persius the satirist.
63 Epistles to Timothy (1) and Titus are written. Josephus is in Rome.
64 Great fire at Rome (July 19) and first imperial persecution of Christians. Festus dies and is succeeded briefly by Albinus then by Gessius Florus.
65 Plot in Rome against Nero. Death of Lucan and Seneca.
66 Great revolt in Palestine. Death of Petronius.
67 Possible date of Paul's arrest and martyrdom. Vespasian takes over in Palestine. Josephus is captured.
68 Nero's suicide (June) and accession of Galba. Qumran is destroyed.
69 'The year of the four emperors.' Assassination of Galba. Accession and death of Otho and Vitellius. Vespasian becomes emperor after wide civil war in northern Italy.
70 Fall of Jerusalem. Quintilian is appointed to a teaching post in Rome.
71 Formal triumph in Rome of Vespasian and Titus over Jews.
73 Last remnant of Jewish revolt is crushed at Masada.
75 Agrippa and Bernice visit Rome. Josephus' *Jewish War* is published this year or next.
76 Birth of Hadrian the future emperor.
77 Pliny's *Historia Naturalis* (?).
79 Death of Vespasian (June). Accession of Titus. Eruption of Vesuvius (Aug. 24). Death of elder Pliny.
80 Colosseum is opened.
81 Death of Titus and accession of Domitian. Tacitus' first writings appear.
86 Climax of Domitian's persecution of the aristocracy. John is on Patmos (?).
89 Plutarch is in Rome.
94 Josephus' *Jewish Antiquities* is published.
95 Execution of Clemens (a cousin of Domitian) and Glabrio (an exconsul), possibly for Christianity.
96 Death of Statius. John's writings, probably written a little earlier, are in the hands of the church. John's death takes place about this time. Domitian is assassinated on Sept. 18. Pliny publishes his letters, and Tacitus prepares his *Historiae* (published in 105).

 98 Tacitus publishes two monographs (*Agricola, Germania*).
100 Younger Pliny is consul.
101 Death of Silius Italicus and Martial.
105 Tacitus's *Historiae.*
111 Pliny writes to Trajan about the Christians in Bithynia.
116 Tacitus's *Annales.* Juvenal begins writing.
120 Suetonius's *Lives of the Caesars.*

EMPERORS OF THE CENTURY

Augustus	27 B.C.–A.D. 14
Tiberius	14–37
Gaius	37–41
Claudius	41–54
Nero	54–68
Galba	68–69
Otho / Vitellius }	69
Vespasian	69–79
Titus	79–81
Domitian	81–96
Nerva	96–98
Trajan	98–117

THE HEROD FAMILY

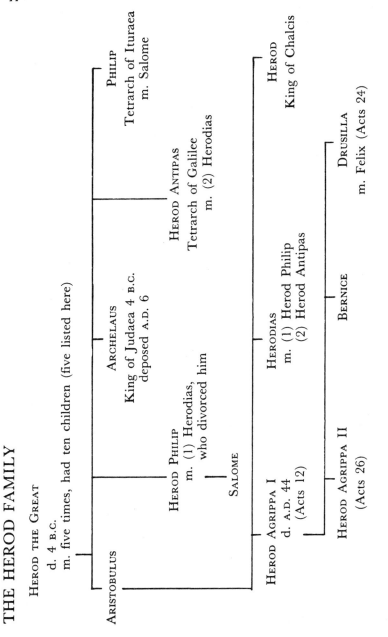

HEROD THE GREAT
d. 4 B.C.
m. five times, had ten children (five listed here)

Notes

CHAPTER 1

1. J. H. Breasted, *History of Egypt*, 2d ed. (New York: Scribner, 1954).
2. Cicero *De Bello Gallico* 4.20–36, 5.8–23.
3. John Bunyan, *The Pilgrim's Progress* (Grand Rapids: Zondervan, n.d.), p. 80.
4. Ernest Renan, *The Life of Jesus* (New York: A. L. Burt, 1863), chap. 25. For comments on Renan's place in the critical succession, see E. M. Blaiklock, *Layman's Answer, an Examination of the New Theology* (Valley Forge, Pa.: Judson, 1969), pp. 77–83.
5. E. M. Blaiklock, 'The Acts of the Apostles as a Document of First Century History,' *Apostolic History and the Gospel, Biblical and Historical Essays Presented to F. F. Bruce* (Exeter: Paternoster, 1970).
6. Tacitus *Annales* 14.52.

CHAPTER 2

1. Tacitus *Annales* 15.44. This passage is examined more closely in Blaiklock, 'The Christian in Pagan Society,' Tyndale New Testament Lecture, 1951.
2. Pliny *Letters* 10.96, 97.
3. For the whole story, see chaps. 10, 11 and 12, of Josephus *Jewish War*, trans. G. A. Williamson (Baltimore: Penguin, 1958).
4. Josephus *Antiquities of the Jews* 18.3.3.
5. Eusebius *Historia Ecclesiastica* 1.11.7.

CHAPTER 3

1. J. B. Phillips, *The Ring of Truth* (London: Hodder & Stoughton, 1967), pp. 31, 32, 76, 77.
2. Adolph Deissman, *The New Testament in the Light of Modern Research* (London: Hodder & Stoughton, 1929), pp. 73–106.
3. See E. M. Blaiklock, *In the Image of Peter* (Chicago: Moody, 1970).
4. Villehardonin & De Joinville, *Memoirs of the Crusades*, ed. Dent, Everyman's Library. These French chroniclers are accessible in this edition to those who find medieval French difficult.

5. E. M. Blaiklock, *Acts: The Birth of the Church*, N. J.: Fleming, Revell, 1980.
6. A Guillaumont & G. Quispel, *The Gospel According to St. Thomas* (London: Collins, 1959). The corruption of truth is apparent on every page of the 'sayings'. For accessible quotations illustrating the point from apocryphal 'gospels,' see E. M. Blaiklock, *Layman's Answer* (Valley Forge: Judson, 1968–69), pp. 67–69.

CHAPTER 4

1. J. B. Phillips, *The Ring of Truth*, pp. 47–48.
2. W. M. Ramsay, *The Cities of St. Paul* (London: Hodder & Stoughton, 1907), pp. 407–418.
3. Ovid *Metamorphoses* 8.618–724.
4. Harry Dansey, *Auckland Star*, 1970. Quoted by kind permission of the author.
5. Phillips, p. 79.
6. Plato *Republic* 2.382D.
7. Plato *Phaedrus* 253Dff.
8. C. S. Lewis, *The Great Divorce* (New York: Macmillan, 1946), p. 89.
9. Plato *Republic* 10.614.

CHAPTER 5

1. W. F. Albright, *The Archaeology of Palestine* rev. ed. (Gloucester, Mass.: Peter Smith, 1971). See all of chapter 11.
2. X. Leon-Dufour, *The Gospels and the Jesus of History* (London: Collins, 1967), p. 67. See also all of chapter 4.
3. Albright, pp. 4, 5.
4. H. T. Frank, *Bible Archaeology and Faith* (New York: Abingdon, 1971), pp. 40, 41, 300–305.
5. Pliny *Letters* 6.16, 20.
6. Xenophon *Anabasis* (The March Up-Country).
7. E. Renan, *Life of Jesus*, pp. 47, 53, 54.

CHAPTER 6

1. John Lawrence in a symposium *We Believe in God* (London: Allen & Unwin, 1968), p. 115.
2. E. M. Blaiklock and D. A. Blaiklock, *Is It or Isn't It* (Grand Rapids: Zondervan, 1968), pp. 70, 71.
3. Arnold Toynbee, *Study of History* (London: Oxford, 1947), 6:278.
4. J. B. Phillips, *Ring of Truth*, pp. 47–48.
5. Purushotman M. Krishna, in *Christianity Today* 28 July, 1972.

CHAPTER 7

1. E. M. Blaiklock, 'The Irony of Paul,' University of Auckland, *Prudentia* 3:1 (May, 1971).
2. Homer *Iliad* 6.440–445.
3. John Milton, *Apology for Smectymnuus* 1.
4. Juvenal *Satires* 10.30ff.
5. Pascal *Pensées* 309.
6. A. J. Hoover, 'Why History? A Defense of God's Revelatory Medium,' *Christianity Today*, July 28, 1972.

CHAPTER 8

1. C. S. Lewis, *Miracles* (New York: Macmillan, 1947), pp. 113, 114.
2. Francis Thompson, *The Hound of Heaven*.
3. Thompson, 'The Kingdom of God' in *Selected Poems* (1908), p. 132.

APPENDIX 1

1. C. C. Dobson, *The Face of Christ* (London: Centenary, 1933).

Index